Torchb

Freedom

The Influence of

RICHARD PRICE

on

EIGHTEENTH CENTURY THOUGHT

By

CARL B. CONE

Published by the UNIVERSITY
OF KENTUCKY PRESS

LEXINGTON

RICHARD PRICE (1723-1791)

By Benjamin West

To Mary Louise

PREFACE

It is surprising how little mention is made of Richard Price in the histories of the last half of the eighteenth century when he was, in fact, one of the better known men of the era. The two previous biographies of Price, by his nephew William Morgan, and by Dr. Roland Thomas, are too brief to do justice to their subject. Neither portrays Price fully enough. My chapters on the American Revolution and the Constitution of the United States, for example, expand events upon which these earlier biographers scarcely touch. The burden of the chapter on the Constitution appeared in the *American Historical Review* (July, 1948), whose editor has kindly consented to the use of that article. I have discussed Price's writings fully because they are not widely read or readily available today and because so much of Price's career was literary.

Among the persons who assisted me in gathering material for this book are Mr. Colton Storm of the William L. Clements Library, Ann Arbor, Michigan; Dr. J. H. Powell; Miss H. J. Williams of the County Library, Bridgend, Glamorganshire, Wales; Mr. D. C. Martin, Assistant Secretary of the Royal Society, London; Mr. Robert F. Metzdorf; and Miss Norma Cass, reference librarian at the University of Kentucky. Mrs. Donald Burt typed the manuscript. The research committee of the University of Kentucky gave me some financial assistance. Dr. J. Merton England, my office mate, offered useful advice, though he doubtless grew tired of hearing about Price.

CARL B. CONE

Lexington, Kentucky
February 17, 1951

TABLE OF CONTENTS

LIST OF ILLUSTRATIONS

CHAPTER I

THE GOOD DR. PRICE

THOSE who best knew him called Richard Price "good." To the cynic the word is soporific, but the cynic has no appreciation for Price's kind anyway. He was a good man in ideas, purpose, and conduct. The best life, he thought, was one dedicated to the service of God, to the fulfillment of God's plan in this world, and to union with God and virtuous men in the next. This did not mean withdrawal from the affairs of the world, passivity, or fatalism. For Price believed that man was God's noblest creature, endowed with free will and empowered to act according to his own choice. If God's purpose was knowable and attainable, its realization might be early or late, depending upon the proper exercise of man's intelligence. Price knew that evil existed, that virtuous conduct did not come easily, that ignorant or unwise men make wrong choices. If men erred, they had only themselves to blame. For revealed religion still contained the essentials of the Divine scheme, and Scripture explained the purposes of human existence. As a dissenting minister Price knew he had the duty to teach these great truths in his sermons, his writings, and the example of his own life.

Price's aim in life was to promote God's works. Unlike those eighteenth century philosophers whose heavenly city was nothing beyond a future earthly community to be built by enlightened secularist sophisticates, with deep humility he found the origin of everything and the destiny of everything in God, the wise and watchful and immediate ruler of the universe. He shared his century's confidence in the steady progress of mankind toward perfection. He thought the world a wonderful place, not a vale of tears. God had not destined man for misery on earth as a preparation for heavenly joys. He had made the world beautiful and He had given to man the capacity for earthly bliss. Price did not disagree with contemporary philosophers about the need for improvement of the world; he only placed the world in a subordinate relationship to Heaven. Earthly happiness, however beautiful, could only be a pale reflection of the supreme felicity of the eternal life.

Nevertheless, Price insisted, it was God's plan for man to attain the perfect life on earth. This perfect life was the free life. Since God wanted man to be free, He bestowed upon him the capacity for enjoying liberty, and gave to him dignity of personality, individuality, a conscience, free will, and intelligence. Thus endowed, man was an autonomous moral agent able to choose the right course and therefore to act virtuously. This moral freedom is the basis for all other freedoms, of which the political and religious are the most significant. But until freedom is complete, the world will remain imperfect, and that is why Price considered it part of his duty to God to promote the cause of freedom throughout the world. Whether, therefore, he wrote a book on moral philosophy, supported the Americans and the French in their revolutions, inveighed against the Test and Corporation Acts, or denounced established churches, it was always because human liberties were involved. At the time of his death in 1791, he was satisfied with the way he had spent his life, for he was sure that the cause of freedom had been perceptibly advanced during the fifty years he had fought for it.

"Fight" is not too strong a word. Along with his "goodness," his gentleness and humility, Price displayed vigor, tremendous courage, and forthrightness. He belonged to a religious minority; he advocated political ideas that were unpopular with the governing class in England during the crises of the American and French revolutions. But he was never intimidated, and confident of the rightness of his views, he boldly and positively advanced them. Consequently he "long stood the object of reproach and calumny to the interested tools of power, to the prejudiced, and to the timid."[1] Few of his enemies, however, could find it possible to accuse him of having interested views. They had to concede the purity and altruism of his efforts, and the complete honesty and sincerity of his beliefs. These qualities of Price's character impressed themselves upon his contemporaries. Even the orange women in the market stalls cried, as they saw his familiar form approaching on the white horse, "Make way! Make way for the good Dr. Price!"

Physically, he was not a prepossessing person. He was small and never robust. His features were strong without being severe, and were even pleasing when he relaxed into quiet humor. Though a preacher by profession, he was not a pulpit orator. His delivery was awkward, his voice unpleasing. Again, it was his strength of character and the thoughtfulness of his sermons that won him success as a minister.

He grew in stature the better one knew him. That is why he had so many friends, among whom were some of the greatest of his contemporaries in England, France, and America. This eighteenth century community of enlightened men, drawn together by kindred interests in political philosophy, science, and letters, had a common faith in the power of human reason, in the perfectibility of man, and in the unrelenting progress of mankind. Price was one of the most respected members of this international fraternity.

The public aspects are the best known parts of Price's life, and his name is mentioned frequently in the memoirs, correspondences, and biographies of the period. Unfortunately, not a great deal has come down to us about the details of his private affairs. People knew him best for his works; the memoir writers concentrated upon these rather than upon intimate, personal matters. Price was not a person about whom anecdotes abound. His personality stands out clearly in the sources, but his private activities are concealed. We

[1] Quoted from Joseph Priestley's funeral oration by the *Gentleman's Magazine*, LXI (1791), part 1, p. 557.

know, for example, that he was happily married, though his wife soon after the marriage became an invalid and never bore children. We know that she was a sweet, intelligent woman, highly regarded by Price's friends. We can assume, without being able to document the statement, that she aided her husband in his work and encouraged him during the difficult early years of his preaching career. But there is no accumulation of incident to aid the biographer in making his subject live.

Partly this is because Price's life was not eventful. He was not a man of action performing deeds of heroism on the battlefield, or even taking a leading part in political life. But if his life was uneventful, it was not uninfluential. Quite the contrary. This quiet little man, laboring night after night in the tower study of his home in Hackney, brought forth books and pamphlets and sermons on a variety of subjects, and thereby fulfilled his duty to God and man. What he wrote and said about moral philosophy, life insurance, the public debt, and politics and religion was important. He is best known to historians for his political writings which, insisted Priestley, "have contributed more than those of any other person, I may almost say living or dead, to make [civil liberties] generally understood, and, what is more, to their importance being truly felt."[2] This praise was not as extravagant as that contained in the obituary notice of the *Gentleman's Magazine*. Balancing the natural fulsomeness of an obituary account is the normal hostility of this periodical toward Price. In any case, this was a contemporary view of Price's place in history.[3] One of the "first philosophers of every age," this friend of man and foe of usurped power was one of the "most distinguished patriots and benefactors of nations." Men loved him for his "excellent understanding, his boldness and freedom of thinking, the purity of his views, and the simplicity of his manners."

This article went on to predict how history would record Price's name with those of Franklin, Washington, Lafayette,

[2] *Ibid.*   [3] *Ibid.*, 389-90.

and Paine. Instead, history has neglected the man who possessed, according to Condorcet, "one of the formative minds of the century." The verdict of history is unjust; Benjamin Franklin would be shocked by it.

CHAPTER II

THE DISSENTING INFLUENCE

THOUGH this is the story of the life of Richard Price, it is also a part of the history of English Dissent, which began in the time of Price's grandfather. Price is not understandable apart from his dissenting heritage and environment. His Presbyterian parents sent him to dissenting schools. After studying in a dissenting academy, he entered the ministry, and for half a century preaching and pastoral care were his regular duties. Many of his dearest friends were dissenting clergymen and laymen. His social and political philosophy, his encouragement of education and science, his fierce and steadfast insistence upon the rights and dignity of the individual, and his hatred of tyranny in any form were in the best traditions of English Dissent. More vocal than most Dissenters of his generation, Price also surpassed them in learning, ability, capacity for friendship, and therefore in contemporary fame and influence.

When Charles II returned to England after the Puritan Revolution, he hoped that Parliament would provide "a liberty to tender consciences." Anglicans, however, felt little kindness toward the Puritan tormentors who had deprived them of political power, banned their church, and forced the sale of their estates to pay the heaviest taxes England had ever known. The election of 1661 returned the vindictive "Cavalier Parliament." And the Anglicans had their revenge. By a series of savage laws, misnamed the Clarendon Code, they reestablished their church and drastically restricted the religious, personal, and political careers of the Protestant Dissenters.

Although these laws were not enforced with uniform zeal, Dissenters suffered wherever magistrates took their executive duties seriously. Thus was created "the martyrology of dissent," and there arose among English Puritans a "political tradition . . . of vigilant criticism and protest towards the powers that rule society and the State."[1]

Among the 2,000 or more clergymen driven out of the Anglican Church by the Act of Uniformity was the Reverend Samuel Jones. A graduate of Oxford, a master classicist, and something of an orientalist as well, he had to abdicate the vicarage of Llangynwyd parish near Bridgend, Glamorganshire, Wales. Many of his parishioners of Presbyterian leanings followed him out of the Church of England and as a new dissenting congregation attended services in Jones' farmhouse, called Brynllywarch. Except for a brief period, which Jones spent in jail, the Clarendon Code was not rigorously enforced in the neighborhood of Bridgend. The congregation at Brynllywarch flourished, and soon two other chapels were established, at Bridgend and at Bettws a few miles to the north. Like so many of his ejected colleagues, Jones recognized the importance of education for dissenting youth. At Brynllywarch he founded an academy to which came also the sons of Anglicans whose dislike of Dissenters did not blind them to the learning and competence of the apostate schoolmaster.

The Prices of Tynton, Llangeinor, a substantial family, were parishioners of the Reverend Samuel Jones. They left the Anglican Church with him, joined his congregation, and gave a farm for the endowment of the Bettws and Bridgend chapels.[2] Rees Price sent his two sons, Rees and Samuel, to the Jones academy to begin preparation for the ministry. The younger son, Samuel, went farther afield, probably because as the younger he had no inheritance. After studying under the able Timothy Jollie in Yorkshire, he came in 1703 to assist

---

[1] G. M. Trevelyan, *England Under the Stuarts* (16th ed , London, 1933), 342. See also an essay by H. G. Plum, *Restoration Puritanism, A Study of the Growth of English Liberty* (Chapel Hill, 1943), especially Chapter II.

[2] Caroline E. Wilhams, *A Welsh Family* (London, 1893), 16.

Dr. Isaac Watts at the hymn writer's chapel in Mark Lane, London.[3] When Watts' health gave way Samuel Price carried most of the pastoral burdens, and after Watts died he was sole pastor for eight years until his own death in 1756. Not a prolific writer, Price won the respect of his London associates for his devotion to dissenting interests.

Rees Price, the father of Richard, was born in 1673 in the farmhouse called Tynton in which the Prices had lived for two hundred years. After becoming a minister he assisted his old mentor Samuel Jones, succeeding him after 1697 as head of both the chapel at Bridgend and the academy. He was a stern person who believed that the elect predestined for salvation were few indeed. His extreme Calvinism alienated the Presbyterian and the Congregational Fund Boards, which cut off support to the academy until William Evans became master and moved it to Carmarthen. The academy suffered other tribulations, but it survived them all. The forerunner of all university education in Wales, it still functions as the Carmarthen Presbyterian College; it is one of the oldest theological seminaries in England.[4]

Though his temperament caused him to fail as a schoolmaster, Rees Price made money from his farms. When he married a girl named Gibbon, her property, of course, came into his possession. Before she died, this first wife bore four children. The second wife of Rees Price was Catherine Richards, the daughter of a Bridgend physician and twenty years younger than her husband. She had three children, Sarah, Richard, and Elizabeth.

Richard was born on February 23, 1723, in Tynton. The house—an unadorned, solid, rectangular structure of two stories, with a gabled roof—reflected the comfortable financial circumstances of the Price family. But the atmosphere within

---

[3] Walter Wilson, *The History and Antiquities of Dissenting Churches and Meeting Houses, in London, Westminster, and Southwark;* . . . (4 vols., London, 1808-1814), I, 319; Arthur Paul Davis, *Isaac Watts, His Life and Works* (Privately printed, 1943), 29-30.

[4] Roland Thomas, *Richard Price, Philosopher and Apostle of Liberty* (Oxford, 1924), 3-4. This book is best for the Welsh background.

the home was unusually austere, even in comparison with other dissenting households in which religion was the constant passion and "The whole family was laid under what they considered to be the restraints of the Gospel."[5] While the proportion decreased as the century passed, many dissenting families held private devotions, including scriptural readings, meditation, prayer, catechizing of children and servants, the reading of a sermon, and the singing of psalms. Rees Price refused to relax any of these offices; to him they were moral duties. Richard's mother, however, is said to have been charming and beautiful. She gave to Tynton whatever grace and lightness it possessed, just as she gave her sweetness of temper to her only son.

Rees Price planned a business career for Richard. According to dissenting lights a good education was essential, no matter what one's calling. Richard's first teacher was a family governess; then he studied under a neighbor youth named Peters, who later entered the ministry. Next, Richard went to a school in Bridgend where he endured a brief period under a schoolmaster who was a kind of Wackford Squeers. Fortunately, his father withdrew him from the school upon learning of the master's nasty temper. Nearby, at Neath, the Reverend Joseph Simmons kept a school, and this Richard attended for the next two years.

At the age of twelve, Richard was ready for an academy not only more advanced but also more distant. He went northwest to Pentwyn in the shire of Carmarthen, where Samuel Jones conducted an academy. This Samuel Jones is not to be confused with the minister of the same name who had died in 1697. Nor is he to be identified with still another Samuel Jones, the most famous of the three, the tutor of the Tewkesbury academy. The Jones under whom Richard studied for the next three years was a minister of Unitarian leanings.

During the eighteenth century, Presbyterianism, once the most numerous Protestant denomination in England, filtered

[5] David Bogue and James Bennett, *History of Dissenters, from the Revolution in 1688, to the year 1808* (4 vols., London, 1808-1812), II, 173.

down into Arianism, Socinianism, Arminianism, and other modifications, and the orthodox Calvinists came to be the least significant of the Protestant communities. Jones' teachings and the readings he recommended bent Richard Price toward Arianism. In particular, the writings of Samuel Clarke, who belonged to the intellectual school of moralists, influenced strongly the theological and ethical beliefs of the teen-age boy. Rees Price disapproved violently of his son's tendency toward theological unorthodoxy. Once when he caught Richard reading Clarke, he angrily snatched away the book and threw it in the fire. There would be no deviations from Trinitarianism in this Presbyterian household.

This incident, which may also have been a discovery to Richard's father, had something to do with the change of schools that took place soon after. Vavasor Griffith, a product of the famous dissenting institution at Tewkesbury, had in 1733 taken over the academy in direct descent from the one founded by Samuel Jones and conducted by Rees Price. For the time being, Griffith and his academy, like a man and his suitcase, were stopping at Talgarth in Breconshire. To this place, forty miles from his home, Richard went in 1738. The annual cost for keeping a pupil in Griffith's school was £5, and that sum covered tuition, room, and board. Griffith was a learned man; his scholars were ably taught.

Throughout the eighteenth century, dissenting academies were the most important feature of English education.[6] At first they depended almost entirely upon the fortunes and lives of their founders, but after 1689, when the Toleration Act enlarged Dissenters' liberties, they rested on more secure foundations, often enjoying the support of permanent funds and outside societies. By the middle of the eighteenth century, the academies were becoming institutionalized, with their own trustees and subscribers. The curricula as well as the character of these academies gradually changed. The first generation of teachers, to which Samuel Jones belonged, included many

[6] H. McLachlan, *English Education under the Test Acts* (Manchester, 1931), 2-4.

men of university background who emphasized classical studies and scholastic methods and used the same textbooks as the universities. Logic and metaphysics, the classical languages, theology, pneumatology, Jewish and Christian antiquities, ethics, Scripture, and mathematics were the chief subjects. The later academies, however, offered various sciences, modern languages, history, and even accounting, shorthand, and elocution. In no dissenting academy, of whatever period, were students pampered. At the age of fifteen Richard Price studied on the university level.

Rees Price died suddenly on June 28, 1739. Most of his property he left to the children of his first marriage, chiefly to John. Richard's share was £400, which he promptly gave over to his mother, for she and Richard's two full sisters had been left to make their way as best they could. Richard remained in school at Talgarth while his mother, having to give up Tynton, moved with her daughters to Bridgend into an old house on the bank of the River Ogwr. Mrs. Price was in poor health during the next winter, and Richard more than once walked the forty miles to visit her.

The year at Talgarth was one of decision for Richard. His inclinations for the ministry were crystallizing, and his reading of Joseph Butler's *The Analogy of Natural and Revealed Religion* influenced him greatly. On June 4, 1740, his tired mother died. This was the last in a chain of events that resulted in his decision to enter the ministry. Uncle Samuel in London promised to help him, and so did his wealthy half-brother John. The assistance of the generous John turned out to be the loan of a horse to carry Richard the twenty miles to Cardiff! Anyway, this was a start. By various means the seventeen-year-old youth made his way to London, entering the city on a broad-wheeled wagon in the autumn of 1740.

Uncle Samuel was true to his word. He found Spartan living quarters for Richard over a barbershop in Pudding Lane, and also furnished money for his nephew's meager needs. The problem of schooling was easily settled. An extremely wealthy Dissenter, William Coward, who died in 1738, left a sum of

£150,000 in a trust fund, the income of which was used both for charitable and educational purposes.[7] Isaac Watts was a member of the Board of the Coward Trust, and Samuel Price lectured under the terms of the fund. Two schools which drew support from the fund, that of Philip Doddridge at Northampton, and the one in London which was commonly known as "Coward's Academy," were actively managed by the Coward Trust. Their students had to pass examinations in the presence of the Trustees and to deliver a sermon in the Bury Street Chapel. Coward's will did not reflect his Calvinism, and though an Arian, Richard Price had no trouble in securing admission to the academy, which during Richard's student days, 1740-1744, was in Tenter-alley, Moorfields. Later it was moved to Hoxton, where it remained until it closed in 1785.

Richard's time in Coward's Academy coincided with the last four years of the life of one of the most erudite men in England. John Eames had studied for the ministry, but it needed only one disappointing sermon to make him realize his unfitness for the pulpit. He was shy and sadly defective "in the powers of elocution." Despite his "harsh, uncouth and disagreeable" pronunciation, he became a remarkably successful teacher. Isaac Watts called him "the most learned man I ever knew." As the only layman ever to have charge of a dissenting academy, he achieved a unique distinction, and he devoted himself to teaching rather than to writing. He had been on the faculty of the academy for nearly thirty years when Price became his student. Although Eames had taught almost every subject in the curriculum, his specialities were science and mathematics. His close friend Isaac Newton introduced him to the Royal Society, which accepted him into its fellowship. Certainly Price acquired his mathematical competence from Eames. For proficiency in mathematics Price once received a gift of £10 from some friend of the academy; he sent the money to his sisters.

[7] Davis, *Isaac Watts*, 53. *Gentleman's Magazine*, VIII (1738), 221, says "the bulk" of Coward's fortune was left to charity.

Price spent the vacation period in 1741 in Bridgend recovering from the jaundice brought on by fatigue from his arduous studies. Returning to London in the autumn, he moved into more comfortable quarters. He went at his studies just as enthusiastically as before. Eames was now in poor health, and much of the teaching burden fell upon James Densham, a man with a fine memory, a passion for system, and the energy to teach—all in one winter—logic, geography, algebra, trigonometry, physics, and conic sections. When he left the academy in 1744, Price had studied the classics, Hebrew, several branches of philosophy, divinity and theology under various special titles, a little oriental lore, mathematics, anatomy, some of the sciences, a practical subject called "pastoral care," and even elocution.

CHAPTER III

CLERGYMAN AND MORALIST

U PON graduating from Coward's Academy, Richard Price was ready to begin his work in the dissenting ministry. For the first time he had to face up to the embarrassments and contradictions, and also the responsibilities, that complicated the life of the Dissenter. The Toleration Act of 1689 allowed Dissenters, but not Roman Catholics or Unitarians, to worship and teach without fear of imprisonment, provided they observed certain formal requirements that were not especially heavy. The Dissenter could inherit property and engage in any business he cared, subject to the exclusions prejudice might raise against him. He could not enter Oxford nor take a degree from Cambridge; municipal and crown offices, and therefore political preferment, could not be his. Admitting these confusions, the legal and social position of the Dissenter was much better than it had been in the days when Price's grandfather chose the dissenting way of life. Although he still met with discrimination and humiliation, the Dissenter of Price's day walked with increasing boldness upon the stage of English life.

Yet persecution had left its marks; it explains in part the Dissenter type. Of whatever denomination, the Dissenter insisted upon the right of private judgment in religious matters. He denied justification under the laws of God for the establishment of any church by man-made statutes. Such individualism inevitably resulted in the fragmentation of English Dissent. In other respects, the Dissenter generally was characterized as an earnest, hardworking, rational, intellectual, and public-spirited person.

No one knows how many Dissenters there were. In the decade before Price's birth, one estimate figured 1,107 congregations in England and 43 in Wales.[1] In 1772 the number for England had declined by fifteen, while that for Wales had quadrupled; a decade after Price died, 1,583 congregations met in England, of which 106 were in the county of Middlesex and 419 in Wales.[2] But out of all proportion to their numbers, Dissenters participated in the liberal political agitations and the movements for humanitarian social reforms that appeared in the eighteenth century. "A large body of the most conscientious and enthusiastic men became political critics and social reformers by profession, for their own wrongs sharpened their sensibility to the wrongs of others, and their own position never permitted them to fall into the sleep of those to whom the world is an easy bed."[3]

Richard Price was one of these men. Not original in his political thought, he was prominent in his time precisely because he emphasized the individualistic liberalism of the rights of man and the right of revolution. He spoke in terms his contemporaries understood and expressed ideals congenial to those who wished to improve the existing order. His clerical position did not bar him from a leading part in the political agitations of his age, for nothing in the dissenting creed prohibited sermons and writings of a political and reforming cast. Rather, when he chose the ministerial career, Price only increased his obligation to work for the betterment of mankind. His choice was a conscious one.

Price was under no illusions, either, about the hardships of the clerical life, for from boyhood he had been intimately connected with it. As a student of religion, he accepted the duty of guiding laymen in the ways of God. He must be prepared always to sacrifice personal interests to pastoral needs. Multifarious as his practical labors among his congregation would be, he must also be a spiritual leader, through prayers

[1] Bogue and Bennett, *History of Dissenters*, II, 98-99.
[2] *Ibid.*, III, 329, *ibid.*, IV, 327-28. Methodist congregations are not included
[3] Trevelyan, *England Under the Stuarts*, 346.

and preaching bringing the word of God into the affairs of a busy world. The sermon must not be taken lightly. It must display erudition, reasoning power, and—not least of all—physical endurance. According to the dissenting practice, the sermon was a thing to be long labored over, carefully composed, and preferably (at the time Price became a minister) written out in full. Dissenters disliked the habits of Methodist preachers who spoke extemporarily. Anyone who has read dissenting sermons must respect the energy, intelligence, and persistence of the dissenting clergy—and the hardihood of their congregations. Another thing Price knew well. The ministerial career was not the way to wealth. A salary of £100 a year was unusually large; the average was about £40.[4] Only devotion to a cause drew men into the ministry or kept them there once they entered.

Price was twenty-one years old when he was ordained to the ministry. Considering his youth and lack of experience he would have been vain to expect the sole charge of a chapel. The dissenting practice allowed a congregation to choose its pastor, and normally a young minister had to serve a term as an assistant until he had earned for himself a reputation to merit a call by some congregation. Upon his uncle's recommendation, Price became family chaplain in the household of a rich Dissenter named Streatfield.

Price lived in Stoke Newington, a pleasant, wooded, suburban area about four miles north of the City of London, and among its thousand residents were many rich Dissenters. The dissenting mind saw no incompatibility between spirituality and affluence. Quite the contrary, for the virtues that made for right living made also for business success. "Early to bed and early to rise" was something more than a nursery rhyme for the Dissenter: hard work and thriftiness were positive duties; card games, dances, and theaters interfered with spiritual and material well-being. The children of dissenting parents, after fearing God, rendered obedience to their elders;

[4] Anthony Lincoln, *Some Political and Social Ideas of English Dissent, 1763-1800* (Cambridge, 1938), 60, n. 3.

the father, dividing his time among chapel, countinghouse, and family circle, attempted to bring with him into the paths of righteousness all who lived under his authority. Professional men, merchants, and manufacturers made up a large proportion of the urban Dissenters. Some of them became persons of great influence and wealth; in the early eighteenth century "a bankruptcy, in a dissenter, was . . . almost unknown."[5]

People called Stoke Newington "the favorite seat of the dissenting muses." The Abney family, with whom Isaac Watts lived for so long a time, included perhaps the best known residents. Sir Thomas Abney, one of the founders of the Bank of England, had been Lord Mayor of London in 1700 and now his spinster daughter, Lady Elizabeth, was the "lady of the manor of Stoke Newington." She and Price became good friends. The banker, Thomas Rogers, also lived in Stoke Newington. Later, when he had his own chapel, Price dwelt only two doors from the Rogers family, who attended his services.

As a family chaplain and private secretary, Price's duties were light. He not only had time for his own scholarly studies, but with Streatfield's consent, he preached before several congregations. In this way he gained the experience and reputation necessary for the holding of a full pastorate. His most important assistantship during these twelve years as a chaplain was at the Old Jewry, the Presbyterian chapel of Dr. Samuel Chandler. Samuel Price, a friend of Chandler, secured the post for his nephew. Chandler, who had studied under Samuel Jones of Tewkesbury, the master of Price's old tutor Vavasor Griffith, was a Biblical scholar and a forceful preacher, with a gift for vivid language. As a "liberal Calvinist," he had no difficulty tolerating his assistant's Arianism. Chandler also supported the periodic agitation for repeal of the Test and Corporation Acts.

Though they agreed on politics and differed only slightly on religion, Price and his superior did not get along well with one another. Tradition blames Chandler for the incompat-

<hr />

[5] Bogue and Bennett, *History of Dissenters*, II, 174.

ibility because he resented the rapid growth of his assistant's popularity among the congregation.[6] Whether true or not, such things have doubtless happened many times in ecclesiastical history. Price's nephew tells a highly improbable story about Chandler that, from one point of view, has a Machiavellian tone. Chandler criticized his assistant's "Methodist" fervency in the pulpit, and Price tried so earnestly to correct his exaggerations that he fell into the opposite fault of restraint. The congregation disliked Price's new manner of preaching, and so Chandler dismissed him. It could be more likely that Chandler was sincerely attempting to help his young assistant, and when his efforts proved futile, he gave up Price as hopelessly inept. In any event, Price never bore ill will toward Chandler. Price was one of a group of dissenting ministers who, after Chandler's death in 1766, purchased his manuscript Biblical criticisms with the intention, never fulfilled, of publishing them.

Actually Price would have been the last to deny contemporary accounts of his lack of grace and fluency in the pulpit. His weak, unpleasant voice accentuated his other shortcomings as a speaker. His later success as a preacher grew out of the thoughtful content of his sermons, the quiet earnestness of his demeanor, and his sincerity and humility. These qualities were magnified by the fame Price later won as a writer. But at the beginning of his career he had a hard time. He had to make his way upon the strength of pulpit performances that at best were awkward.

Price studied hard during his tenure of the chaplaincy. He was a slow, methodical worker. He read carefully rather than widely and superficially, taking elaborate notes upon his readings and pondering over them afterwards. The fruits of these labors appeared in his writings.

Price had time for his studies also because he had no distracting family obligations. His sisters were married and living in Wales. Already Price had formed the habit of returning to Wales nearly every summer to visit his relatives. He held

---

[6] Wilson, *Dissenting Churches*, II, 384.

no grudge even against his magnanimous half-brother John, whose daughter was Price's favorite niece. Of his two sisters in Bridgend, the older one, Sally, was married to a physician, William Morgan, who had succeeded Price's maternal grandfather in medical practice. Two of their sons, William and George Cadogan, were to figure prominently in their uncle's life in later years.

Price always enjoyed moderate physical exercise as a means of preserving his health. He preferred horseback riding and sea-bathing. He was a strong swimmer, yet once near Brighton the ocean almost captured him. At Paradise Row in the New River he had an embarrassing experience; after heroically hauling a drowning man out of the water, he discovered to his dismay that he had only interfered with a suicide. Price also liked walking in the country. On one of his jaunts a robber forced him to give up his shoe buckles. But Price was not intimidated; he lectured the fellow sternly for engaging in such a "bad business." For once Price may have amused his audience.

In 1756 both Streatfield and Uncle Samuel died, and each left Price a legacy. The money from the one and the house in Leadenhall Street from the other made Price financially secure. He lived simply and never cared for money as such, but neither did he have to worry about not having enough. He always gave gladly to charity, practicing his doctrine of Christian benevolence. His friend, Joseph Priestley, emphasized Price's generosity.[7] He ought to have known, for Price helped finance some of his scientific experimentation. Priestley said that Price lived so frugally, without being miserly, that always he had an annual surplus from his modest income. Price regularly gave a fifth of his income to charity.

About the time he became financially independent, Price fell in love. How he met the young lady is not recorded, but the acquaintance resulted in love at first sight. Sarah Blundell's father, a wealthy speculator, had lost most of his money when the South Sea Bubble burst. He salvaged enough, however,

---

[7] *Gentleman's Magazine*, LXI (1791), part 1, p. 558.

to leave Sarah a few thousand pounds and the house in Cheapside in which she was living at the time she met Price. They were married in Stoke Newington on June 16, 1757, probably, as required by the Hardwicke Marriage Act of 1753, according to the rites of the Anglican Church. For the next year they resided on a noisy street in Hackney, a suburb about two miles northeast of the City. Sarah remained a communicant of the Established Church, though she had married a dissenting minister who was not even a Trinitarian. Religious toleration was not an academic subject for Price; he practiced it in his own household. Never in strong health, Mrs. Price bore no children.

Sometime during these early years Price wrote one of his most eloquent passages. More succinctly than anything else it states his credo and reveals the person his contemporaries knew him to be: *"Beauty and wit* will die, *learning* will vanish away, and all the *arts of life* be soon forgot; but *virtue* will remain forever. This unites us to the whole rational creation, and fits us for conversing with any order of superior natures, and for a place in any part of God's creation."

This sentiment occurred almost at the end of the book which Price published in 1758. His first work, it established him as a moral philosopher. The book is important in understanding the man, for the views it contains remained the basis not only of his ethical conduct, but of his political philosophy. He had been working at the book off and on since his student days; he said in the preface to the first edition that he had revised it several times. Published by the firm of A. Millar and T. Cadell —Cadell handled all of Price's subsequent writings—the book was entitled *A Review of the Principal Questions and Difficulties in Morals, particularly those respecting the origin of our Ideas of Virtue, its Nature, relation to the Deity, Obligation, Subject-matter, and Sanctions.*[8]

8 A corrected second edition appeared in 1769 and a third, enlarged with "A Dissertation on the Being and Attributes of the Deity," came out in 1787. References will be to the third edition, whose title omits the words "and Difficulties." D. Daiches Raphael, the editor of a new edition based on Price's

Price's concern throughout his life was with the question of human freedom, and quite naturally he conceived it his primary task to prove the objectivity of moral judgments. In this he agreed with Francis Hutcheson, but for the most part he had to refute the views expressed in Hutcheson's posthumous *System of Moral Philosophy* (1755) and in David Hume's skeptical, devastating *Inquiry into the Principles of Morals* (1751). These empiricists held that even moral ideas were derived from sense perceptions, and that the test of good and evil in an act was the manner in which it affected us. This, for Price, was a crucial struggle, for if empiricism triumphed, then relativism would hold the lists. Philosophy and religion would be divorced, and there would be no place in morality for God. In opposition to the empiricists, Price adhered to the tradition of Ralph Cudworth and Samuel Clarke, believing that "the Cartesian intuition of self-evident truths is to be found in our awareness of moral principles."[9] Reason alone perceived moral distinctions; the rightness or wrongness of actions was determined a priori rather than in terms of consequences. Having rejected utilitarianism and its parent empiricism, Price had to clarify his own theory of the origin of ideas, and rightly, his approach was neither psychological nor metaphysical, but epistemological.[10] Of his epistemology, he frankly stated in the preface to his first edition that "If I have failed here, I have failed of my purpose."

Price boldly attacked the empiricist theory of the origin of ideas, particularly that of John Locke. By arguments today recognized as extremely acute, he showed that sensationalism could not account for moral truths. The moral sense was not blind instinct nor was the end of moral action hedonistic self-satisfaction. Moral judgments were acts of intellection, and moral principles were not derived from sense perception.

---

third (Oxford, 1948), has contributed a splendid introduction on Price's moral philosophy.

[9] Raphael (ed.), *Price's Review of Morals*, xiv.

[10] W. H. F. Barnes, "Richard Price — A Neglected 18th Century Moralist," *Philosophy*, XVII (1942), 160.

The moral faculty Price lodged in the understanding. Because it furnished the mind a priori with general ideas or universals, the understanding was the faculty that apprehended objective truth. Price thus held that moral ideas were simple—derived from the understanding—though in Locke's view simple ideas came immediately from sense perception. Such universal ideas as truth and reality lay beyond the scope of sense, and "that philosophy [Hume's, for example] cannot be very inviting, which thus explodes all independent truth and reality (because sense does not perceive them), resolves knowledge into particular modifications of sense and imagination, and makes these the measure of all things."[11] In Plato and Cudworth Price found much ammunition for his attack on sensationalism, but his account of moral objectivity was his own distinct, original, and noble contribution to moral philosophy.[12]

However intimately he associated morality with understanding or reason, Price could not exclude emotion or esthetic feeling from moral judgments. Even though good and evil were objective, man felt a certain "moral beauty" in right actions, and to do wrong was odious. Both understanding and sense could be delighted or offended by human actions, and these faculties worked together in discerning right and wrong. The understanding remained supreme, however, for beauty and deformity were subjective; they admitted of degrees; they were caused by the objective good and evil which were in the moral acts themselves.[13] Actions were not motivated by desire for pleasure or fear of pain; the yearning for happiness was ever present, but only the understanding revealed the real nature of happiness and misery. Instinctive amiability, devoid of thought, characterized the brute.[14] At the other end of the scale, the intelligent being saw that virtue did not lie in hedonistic self-interest, but rather in perceiving the rightness of

[11] *Review*, 43.

[12] Both Raphael and Barnes say Sir Leslie Stephen's judgment, expressed in his *History of English Thought in the Eighteenth Century* (London, 1872), which struck me as agnostically unsympathetic toward Price, is unfair and lacking in understanding.

[13] *Review*, Chapter II.   [14] *Ibid.*, 114, 122.

God's plan and man's duty to follow that plan. Morality could not be independent of God nor truth of the nature of God, for God was eternal Mind.[15]

From the nature of morality Price turned to the manifestations of morality in human conduct.[16] To the thinking man, virtue was obligatory. The first of its several aspects was duty to God, which was so fundamental that it ought to govern our lives and all our actions. Duty to God took the outward form also of gratitude to Him for blessings, and a proper reverence. Then followed duty to oneself, benevolence, gratitude, veracity, and justice in our dealings with others. When these parts of virtue clashed, or seemed to, one should choose his course of action according to the immutable principles of morality. The choice itself was an act of volition; that was why one must study morality, for only the informed man could choose rightly and knowingly and thus act virtuously. This very freedom of choice contained the possibilities of error, for if the rules of morality never changed, yet their practical application might vary according to time and circumstances.[17] In recognizing "practical virtue," Price faced the same problem as the utilitarians who were to dominate English moral philosophy in the century to come, but he rejected the compromise of relativism.

Without freedom, or the power to form decisions and act, Price continued, there could be no moral capacity.[18] This liberty, obviously, could be dangerous, but how much better it was to be free, even to err, than to be the creature of physical necessity! Price was never oblivious to this problem, as his later writings showed, though in his treatment of morals he rather sensed than stated clearly the contradictions involved in the ideas of moral freedom and natural necessity. Thereby he fell short of the treatment Kant was to give this problem in his third antinomy. Yet human freedom was always at the heart of Price's thoughts and acts. Just as there should be moral autonomy, there should be political and religious

15 *Ibid.*, Chapter IV.   16 *Ibid.*, 171-78, 217-96.
17 *Ibid.*, 295-96.   18 *Ibid.*, 305.

liberty. Without understanding the emphasis Price placed upon freedom of action and will, one misses the integration of his moral, religious, and political thought. Price's dissenting background helped make him an apostle of civil liberty; yet had he not been ardent for freedom he would have denied the implications of his moral philosophy. His view of the nature of man and of man in society was whole and consistent. Virtue could not exist when human actions were determined by physical necessity. Likewise, there could be no political freedom in a community that did not govern itself by laws of its own making or made by a legislature fairly elected by the community.[19] And liberty would be incomplete unless, in addition to enjoying moral autonomy and the right to participate in political life, all men could worship as they pleased, without penalty or discrimination. But first and basic was moral freedom, because virtue would remain long after the "arts of life" were forgotten.

Who, then, was the virtuous man, and how did one recognize him? Price's description depicted the ideals he always tried to uphold. To him, as to Plato, the good man was the one in whom the rational faculty dominated. A man who was ruled by the love of God and of his fellow men and who cherished rectitude would be marked as a good man by the character of his thoughts and deeds. He strove constantly to improve himself, never forgetting that right and wrong were distinctions to be found in the nature of things and that moral obligations were a part of eternal truth. This conception was more difficult to apprehend than the empiricist belief that moral judgments were merely relative to circumstances and human feelings. But it was also much loftier and, as Price expounded it, required deep and abiding faith in the wisdom and goodness of God, the ruler of the universe. For in morals, and in politics which was a branch of morals, the ultimate sanction was God.

[19] Richard Price, *Observations on the Nature of Civil Liberty, the Principles of Government, and the Justice and Policy of the War with America* . . . (London, 1776), part 1, sec. 1.

Price's theory of the foundations of morals, with its insistence that moral action was governed by the intellect of the moral agent, anticipated Kant and his categorical imperative. It is difficult to believe that Kant never read Price, yet there is no direct evidence of his ever acknowledging an obligation to the Englishman. Nevertheless Kant's ethics was a development of Price's. Hastings Rashdall, who considers Price's *Review* "the best work published on Ethics till quite recent times," says rather extravagantly that the book "contains the gist of the Kantian doctrine without Kant's confusions."[20] Without subscribing to so strong a statement, one may still admit a striking general resemblance between their positions, though details show considerable variation and Kant went beyond what Price attempted.

Recently, philosophers have been turning to Price with renewed interest and appreciation after a century and a half of relative neglect. In denying that utilitarianism provides a satisfactory basis for an ethical system, Price had placed himself outside the main stream of English moral philosophy, while the German idealists took Kant as their point of departure, apparently unaware of Price's contributions. Present day intuitionists, such as W. D. Ross and G. E. Moore, have resumed Price's task of proving moral objectivity. Where Price combated the empiricism of Locke, Hutcheson, and Hume, they contend against the results of modern psychology, some of which have shaken the faith in human reason that the eighteenth century possessed. If irrationalism has gone too far, perhaps the "rationalism of Richard Price may yet again be thought worthy of attention."[21]

Though Price was not of pivotal importance in the history of moral philosophy, his ethical theories and writings were not wasted. His *Review* went through three editions in thirty years, which indicated a continued interest in the book. Contemporaries always thought of him as a moralist, even after he earned recognition as an authority upon other

[20] *The Theory of Good and Evil* (2 vols., 2d ed., Oxford, 1924), I, 80-81 n.
[21] Barnes, "Richard Price," *Philosophy*, XVII, 172.

subjects. His congregations and his dissenting friends admired his steadfastness in practicing in his daily life the principles of right living toward which his philosophy led him. Love of God and charity to his fellow men were his ruling passions.

But Price's moral philosophy was more than a guide to his personal conduct. The emphasis upon human freedom as an essential ingredient of morality was the basis for claiming freedom for man in all his aspects. The eighteenth century emphasized the dignity and worth of the individual, and this insistence upon a decent respect for the human personality underlay the revolutionary political ideas of the era. Sometimes, however, these ideas were utilitarian and therefore relative, or else secular and devoid of Divine sanction. It is true that the rights of man were often attributed to God, but the God of many of the revolutionaries was little more than a figure of speech. The "Nature's God" of the Declaration of Independence was a vague and uncertain quality; Price's God was the living, vital, immediate, and positive ruler of the universe.

Here precisely is where Price rose above so many of the political theorists of his time. His political thought came directly out of his moral philosophy; therefore political freedom rested upon moral foundations; and both were of Divine origin. This belief gave depth and stability to Price's thought. Long after the social contract theory was ridiculed by English utilitarians, Price's reasons for claiming freedom as an inalienable right would still be valid. Though he could never be a theocrat, politics was not a secular matter for Price, even when he insisted upon religious freedom and inveighed against state churches. Divine law and God's plan transcended denominational definitions. Price brought God into the affairs of man, or rather, he refused to render lip service to God while excluding Him from the world. No wonder his American friends, so many of whom were clergymen, venerated Price and thought him a great philosopher. For Price's philosophy justified their revolution as a Divinely ordained struggle for human freedom.

Whatever the significance of Price's moral philosophy, his book made him immediately well known. It helped him earn the friendship of some of the leading intellectuals, including the great Hume. In fact, Hume appreciated Price's efforts to blast his skepticism, for as a logician he simply had to proceed from his premises to his conclusions, and he was not at all happy over the spectacular and appalling effects of his skepticism upon both philosophy and religion. Then too, he welcomed Price's gentlemanly tone and conduct. He asked the publisher Cadell to invite to dinner as many as possible of his literary opponents. Besides Price and Hume, Dr. William Adams, Master of Pembroke College, Oxford, and Dr. John Douglas, Bishop of Salisbury, attended.[22] The two philosophers, one a Scot and the other a Welshman, liked one another and visited back and forth, carrying on their philosophical controversy genially and privately. In some of his later writings also Price contested with Hume, but he generously admitted the beneficial influence Hume had upon him.

[22] Samuel Rogers, *Recollections of the Table-Talk of Samuel Rogers* (New York, 1856), 106. Rogers was the son of Price's neighbor, Thomas Rogers.

CHAPTER IV

PRICE IN THE PULPIT

IN 1758 the Prices moved from bustling Hackney to placid Stoke Newington, where Price was handier to the chapel on the Green, which he had been serving as morning and afternoon preacher for two years. Here Price lived for nearly thirty years in a house with a courtyard flanked by an arched entrance through which he rode his well known white horse. The house also had a little turret chamber that made an ideal study where Price labored on his sermons and his other varied projects.

During the 1760's Price held other pastorates before he became permanently established. In December, 1762, he accepted a call as evening preacher to the Presbyterian congregation in Poor Jewry Lane, and so he gave up the afternoon service at Stoke Newington. Unfortunately, the Poor Jewry congregation, like some others of this period suffering from rampant individualism, was splitting into fragments. Shortly after Price accepted the charge of this uneasy chapel, he rejected an invitation from the large Presbyterian congregation at Lewin's Mead, Bristol. His wife's ill health and his own preference for the intellectually stimulating environment of London explain his refusal. Like Samuel Johnson, he felt that not to live in London, the literary as well as the political capital of England, would be not to live where he could be happiest.

Yet Price was not entirely happy during these early years of his ministerial career. He was morose over the results of his preaching. His congregations did not blame their pastor; he was doing his best so far as the content of his discourses went.

But Price was not a good speaker. He lacked warmth. His delivery was rather casual, on the surface, and he seemed to communicate little more than a kind of cold intellectualism to his audiences. A person hearing him for the first time might go away disappointed, particularly one accustomed to exterior elegance in public speakers, for this was an age of great orators.

Nor did his appearance enhance his pulpit presence. He was shorter than average, and thinly built, though his features were strong. He had a determined chin, a nose both long and large, and heavy, black brows. In a small group, however, one noticed the firmness of his visage. And in parlor conversation Price shone. When the subjects interested him, and many did, his features lighted up, his eyes grew bright, and he talked with animation, at the same time displaying such nervous mannerisms as turning his wig on his temples, folding and refolding his cocked hat, or twisting one leg around the other. His wig covered hair that became gray when Price was in his thirties. The story says that his hair changed color during a single night when he was concentrating furiously upon a problem in mathematics. All this does not add up to a fierce looking man, yet the Duchess of Bedford expected him to be that when she met him at Shelburne House.

Conscious of his defects as a pulpit speaker, Price was also aware of what seemed to be evidences of failure as a minister. His experiences at the Poor Jewry Chapel were disheartening, for he was unable to restore unity to the fractious congregation. There was little better prospect of success in Newington. His flock was small; it diminished further as death carried away the older members and few new ones were added. Price even entertained thoughts of giving up during these discouraging early years, but repeatedly he rejected them because he believed in the importance of the ministry. He was sure he could do more good in that calling than in any other. And so he persisted, wisely as it turned out. For, whatever first impressions might be, Price wore well. Gradually his congregations grew accustomed to his awkwardness,

and overlooked it altogether as they became impressed with
the messages of his sermons, their good sense and optimism.
Inexorably his nobility of character shone through, and people
found themselves inspired with the desire to emulate his
goodness.

In 1770 Price's faith in himself was vindicated. He was
asked to become morning preacher at the Gravel-Pit Meeting
House in Hackney. This congregation was larger than the
one in Stoke Newington and more harmonious than the one
at Poor Jewry Lane. To be called to this important pastorate
was a mark of recognition. Price accepted the invitation with
alacrity. He resigned at Poor Jewry Lane, whose congregation
dissolved four years later, and shifted the Stoke Newington
service from morning to evening. The call proved that Price
had risen to a leading position among dissenting ministers.
By the time of the American Revolution his churches over-
flowed, and people came to hear him not just because they
approved of his political views or admired his learning.

Price's wholesome influence upon his associates was described by Samuel Rogers. The families of Thomas Rogers
and Price were intimate socially, and often, after dinner, Price
in his dressing gown dropped in at the Rogers' home for a
chat. Samuel, who was born in 1763, remembered how Price
"would talk and read the Bible, to us, till he sent us to bed
in a frame of mind as heavenly as his own."[1] In these moments
young Samuel Rogers knew he wanted to be a preacher when
he grew up. Instead he became something of a poet and one
of the cultured middle class of early Victorian England. But
Price's influence upon him remained. To be sure, Price demonstrated scientific instruments such as the electrical machine
given him by the Equitable Assurance Society, which he
advised on actuarial matters; he helped the Rogers boys with
their lessons and took part in their games. More important,
Price imparted to Samuel Rogers a philosophy of life, which
Rogers' poem "Human Life" expressed. In his most ambitious
poem, "The Pleasures of Memory," Rogers described his

[1] Rogers, *Table-Talk*, 4.

happy boyhood under the inspiration of Price, Joseph Priestley, Andrew Kippis, and other prominent Dissenters.

> Guides of my life! Instructors of my youth!
> Who first unveil'd the hallow'd form of Truth;
> Whose every word enlighten'd and endear'd,
> In age beloved, in poverty revered;[2]

And

> They in their glorious course the guides of Youth,
> Whose language breathed the eloquence of Truth;
> Whose life, beyond perceptive wisdom, taught,
> The great in conduct, and the pure in thought.[3]

Rogers believed that Price was "one of the gentlest and purest spirits the eighteenth century produced."[4]

Price loved children, and they understood instinctively the sincerity of his affection for them. He placed himself upon their level and led them by winning their confidence. He laid aside ministerial decorum and enjoyed their sports. Once he won a hopping match at Stoke Newington. Another time, in the Rogers' garden, he tried to leap over a bush, and fell in the middle of it, and got up laughing as heartily as the Rogers children. Another of his youthful admirers, destined to achieve fame and notoriety, was Mary Wollstonecraft, who became as ardent an advocate of political liberty as Price could have hoped. As a girl she sat in the pew next to the Rogers' in the Newington chapel.

Price's book on morals and his devotion to ministerial duties enhanced his reputation among Dissenters. Gradually he was drawn into the wider range of dissenting life, though sometimes he refused to assume responsibilities for which he felt himself unfitted, or for which he did not have the time. He declined a tutorship in Coward's Academy, then being moved

[2] Samuel Rogers, *The Poems of Samuel Rogers, with a Memoir* (New York, n.d.), 295-96.

[3] *Ibid.*, 317.

[4] P. W. Clayden, *The Early Life of Samuel Rogers* (London, 1887), 119.

to Hoxton, in the spring of 1762, despite the urgings of his friends Andrew Kippis and Abraham Rees, who were on the faculty. About the same time he refused to edit a new edition of Newton's works for some enterprising booksellers. Price doubted his ability to do a thorough job, though his mathematical attainments were considerable, as the public would soon learn. He did join the board for administering the trust established by Dr. Daniel Williams. Like the Coward Trust, this one provided for the education of dissenting ministers. It also furnished assistance to preachers and their widows, and supported the library that still functions in London.

Among these activities, Price's clerical duties took first place. In addition to preaching, the dissenting minister had what amounted almost to an obligation to write something on theology. Up to 1767, however, Price published only one work on religion, a short sermon in 1759 entitled *Britain's Happiness and the Proper Improvement of It*. The pamphlet attracted scarcely any attention.[5]

In 1767 Cadell published a collection of Price's sermons. Fearing that his preaching was still ineffective, Price had recast some of his discourses, which he always delivered from manuscript, and brought them out in a book entitled *Four Dissertations*.[6] These sermons well deserve a brief summary. Remember, Price was a minister. For fifty years, about three

[5] After Price's death, a person who called himself "A British Manufacturer" wrote an introduction and republished this sermon under the title *Britain's Happiness and Its Full Possession of Civil and Religious Liberty briefly stated and proved*. The sermon had some relevance, despite its age, to the reform controversy then raging in England. Horace Walpole mentioned it in a letter of July 17, 1791, to Mary Berry, and detesting Price, Walpole spoke sneeringly of it as an old sermon of Price's. By this time Price was famous and the pamphlet earned some notice. It was mentioned in the St. James *Chronicle*, the London *Chronicle*, and the *Times*. W. S. Lewis (ed.), *The Yale Edition of Horace Walpole's Correspondence* (New Haven, Conn., 1937-   ), XI, 315 and n. 16.

[6] The four parts are called respectively, "On Providence"; "On Prayer"; "On the Reasons for expecting that virtuous Men shall meet after Death in a State of Happiness"; "On the Importance of Christianity, the Nature of Historical Evidence, and Miracles." Five editions were printed, in 1767, 1768, 1772, 1777, and 1811. References are to the first.

times a week, he preached sermons that were the product of
arduous preparation and not the offspring of an inspiration
that came at the mounting of the pulpit. These sermons tell
much about Price's thought and indicate the depth of the
spiritual messages delivered to his congregations. They further illuminate the moral principles he tried to live by.

In the sermon "On Providence" Price attacked the fashionable view of God the Clockmaker who wound the machinery
and let the universe run ever afterward without supervision.
On the contrary, nature was constantly under the wise direction of a particular Providence whose existence the general
laws and constitution of the universe proved. "The course
of nature is nothing but his power, exerting itself everywhere
according to fixt rules, in order to answer the best ends."[7]
No mechanical explanation that omitted the possibility of
Divine intervention sufficed; like morals and politics, all material causes returned to God as first mover. Price believed
firmly in the Newtonian cosmology.

Difficulties in understanding the operation of Providence
or in reconciling apparent inconsistencies existed only because
finite man could not comprehend the design of God. "We must
therefore be much in the dark."[8] Nevertheless God gave man
the means of attaining happiness, which arose from the
"proper exercise" of human powers and was a matter of free
choice. In accepting Providence, man received many blessings,
for Providence supported morality and encouraged virtuous
action. This doctrine illustrates Price's theological optimism,
so attractive to his listeners.

Price believed mightily in the powers of prayer. Among
Dissenters he had a reputation for inspiring public praying.
He spent an hour daily in self-examination and private prayer,
and longer on the Sabbath. So sincere himself, he was impatient with people who, ostentatious in their public devotions,
neglected ordinary social duties. For he believed prayer to
be a solemn address to God, the Governor of the world. We
ought to acknowledge dependence upon God, to thank Him

---

[7] *Four Dissertations*, 173-74.   [8] *Ibid.*, 159-60.

for His mercies, to confess our sins, and to request happiness for ourselves and others.[9] We ought to pray regularly, in a "plain, serious and simple" manner.[10] Though no one could know how efficacious praying might be, it was not absurd to think that prayer was an action God noticed in communicating good to His creatures. Price saw nothing wrong in appealing to the self-interest of his readers by suggesting the prudence of being on the safe side. This gambler's argument for right living had appeared in the conclusion to Price's *Review of Morals.*

In contrast with the gloom Price displayed in some of his works on worldly affairs, he was cheerful about the promises of virtue rewarded. The evidence from Scripture and religious history gave assurance that good men would recognize their earthly friends in Heaven. Therefore we should not only live virtuously, but we should cultivate the friendship of good people. This was a comforting doctrine. As late as June 9, 1813, in America, Timothy Pickering wrote to his dying friend James McHenry, "In a volume of dissertations by Dr. Price, there is one on the happiness of those who were friends in this world, meeting together in another. It is a most pleasing, cheering & animating discourse."[11]

Having hinted at the subject earlier in the book, Price took up in more detail the matter of miracles. Hume and others had shockingly and convincingly discredited the nature of the evidence for believing in miracles, and a lively controversy still was going on when Price published his *Four Dissertations.* Price began with a statement of his faith, a premise Hume had already challenged. After that he argued doggedly. To be sure, miracles contradicted experience, as Hume had shown, but who was man to speak of experience per se? A miracle was only an event that differed from our previous experience, and in that sense all new phenomena of nature might just as

---

[9] *Ibid.,* 198.   [10] *Ibid.,* 304.

[11] Bernard C. Steiner, *The Life and Correspondence of James McHenry* (Cleveland, 1907), 603-604.

well be called miracles because they were novelties. While nature was fairly regular in her activities, one could not say that the future would be like the past, but only that miracles, while improbable and unpredictable, were not impossible. Here Price returned to faith and rested his argument upon the divine origin of Scripture and the omnipotence of God.

This solacing and optimistic book was well received. It added nothing to theology, but it did contain "some practical exhortations of more than the usual animation of the period."[12] Hume took the attack upon himself graciously. In the first edition Price called Hume's argument "poor sophistry." When he sent a copy to Hume, he apologized for the rudeness of the expression and promised to delete it from later editions. The next year he sent a copy of the corrected second edition to Hume, who wrote to Price expressing "wonder at such scrupulosity in one of Mr. Price's profession."[13] Hume was a veteran polemicist. He had been spitefully and ungenerously attacked by many opponents from among the clergy, and he was pleased that one clergyman, at least, could be a Christian when engaged in literary controversy.

The book engaged the attention of the Earl of Shelburne, who read a good deal of theology. He arranged for Mrs. Elizabeth Montagu, a mutual friend, to introduce him to Price. From this came a lifelong friendship between the peer and the dissenting clergyman.[14] At their first meeting, Shelburne expressed sympathy for the Dissenters and promised assistance to the incipient movement for parliamentary repeal of the legal disabilities under which Dissenters still lived. Shelburne lived up to his promise, but the Test and Corporation Acts remained on the statute books long after Price and Shelburne were dead.

12 Stephen, *English Thought in the Eighteenth Century,* I, 429.

13 William Morgan, *Memoirs of the Life of the Rev. Richard Price, D.D., F.R.S.* (London, 1815), 24. Morgan was Price's nephew, and put into his inadequate biography some information derived from personal knowledge.

14 Lord Edmond George Fitzmaurice, *Life of William, Earl of Shelburne* (3 vols., London, 1875), II, 236.

One other thing the book did for Price. It earned for him the D.D. degree from Marischal College, Aberdeen, on August 7, 1767.[15] Henceforth, he was to be best known simply as Dr. Price.

[15] Thomas, *Price*, 43 and n. 1, correcting Morgan, who said (p. 42) that Price received his degree from Glasgow.

Chapter V

MATHEMATICS AND LIFE
INSURANCE

D URING these years when Price was laboriously and steadily increasing his reputation as a minister, a moral philosopher, and a writer of comforting sermons, he was also busy with other studies. Ever since his student days under John Eames, mathematics had fascinated him. He occasionally challenged himself with mathematical problems as a kind of exercise without particular purpose. Then, quite by accident, he was invited to turn his talents to work upon the doctrine of chances. The immediate fruit of this labor was election to membership in the Royal Society, which brought him into a circle of friendships beyond the dissenting realm. Another result was engrossment with the complexities of mathematical probability, with the related problems of life expectancy and annuities, and finally with the mysteries of the national debt. As his knowledge of these increased, his fame grew, even in America and France, until many thought of Dr. Price as one of the greatest living authorities upon life insurance and public finance.

In April, 1761, Price's friend, the Reverend Thomas Bayes, died. Among his manuscripts were some papers containing mathematical calculations which the relatives asked Price to examine and prepare for publication. One problem that had concerned Bayes was the doctrine of chances. Price completed the work and with a letter dated November 10, 1763, he sent Bayes' paper and his own supplement to John Canton, a member of the council of the Royal Society. These were

read before the society a month later and published in its
Philosophical Transactions under the title, "An Essay toward
solving a Problem in the Doctrine of Chances."[1]

The problem was stated thus: "*Given* the number of times
in which an unknown event has happened and failed [to
happen]: *Required* the chance that the probability of its
happening in a single trial lies somewhere between any two
degrees of probability that can be named."[2] The rule established by Bayes was a long mathematical formula, which
Price had tested.[3] At the end of his remarks Price cautioned
that the solution did not give exactness but only the limits
between which probability lay. The essay contained two other
rules, as modifications of the first one.

A year later Price submitted another paper called "A Dem-
onstration of the Second Rule in the Essay towards the Solution of a Problem in the Doctrine of Chances, published in
the *Philosophical Transactions*, Vol. LIII."[4] This second essay
attempted to show that Bayes' solution did not sufficiently
narrow the limits of the degrees of probability. Though the
work was Bayes', Price put it into presentable form and had
it published. And on December 5, 1765, Price was elected
Fellow of the Royal Society, where interest in science made
denominational differences seem insignificant.

Bayes probably thought of the calculus of chances as a
matter of scientific curiosity. It has since developed into a
considerable study important to many fields of investigation.
As a Newtonian, Price viewed the universe as a wonderful
example of Divine planning, and in that broad sense he saw
the connection between mathematics and philosophy. Although most of his mathematical labors concerned the doc-

[1] LIII (1763), Essay LII, 370-418.   [2] *Ibid.*, 376.

[3] *Ibid.*, 399. This was the rule for the calculation of a posteriori (inductive)
probabilities. Though later mathematicians criticized it, according to Arne
Fisher, *The Mathematical Theory of Probabilities* (New York, 1922), 80, the
rule is theoretically true and under proper conditions will give true results in
practice. Fisher (p. 13) calls it "a very important stepping stone in our whole
theory," and he says it has been carelessly applied.

[4] *Philosophical Transactions*, LIV (1764), Essay LII, 296-325.

trine of probability, Price had no vision of the later particular application of probability to the discipline of logic. He did, however, understand the relation of the rules of probability to calculations of life expectancy, and when his aid was enlisted by a group of men interested in problems of life insurance and mortality tables, he turned his abilities in that direction and applied his knowledge of the rules to good account. Once involved with annuities, he had to deal with statistics, and altogether his work on annuities, mortality tables, population, and public finance emphasized the need for statistics, demonstrated methods of handling them, and encouraged the scientific spirit insofar as it embodied demands for ample and exact data.

In order to understand Price's part in the history of annuities and statistics, one need go back no further than 1662, when John Graunt published his pamphlet on the London bills of mortality. The Royal Society then encouraged similar studies in which Sir William Petty took a leading part. Presently other men began compiling and interpreting social statistics. They found to their dismay that English records were local in character and haphazardly kept. The incomplete parish registers dated from the sixteenth century; the London bills began in 1605, but as they merely summarized the parish registers they perpetuated defects. Several other towns kept variegated records. There were also available in Price's time some private compilations kept by interested clergymen and physicians, as well as the returns from certain taxes, such as the window tax.[5]

Obviously only tentative conclusions could be framed out of such scattered data. The early statisticians made errors while creating a new science. They worked with inadequate information and they had to establish fundamental principles and rules of procedure as they went along. Their dogmatism, which Price shared, and readiness to believe in the complete validity of their ideas were less excusable than their mistakes.

[5] M. C. Buer, *Health, Wealth, and Population in the Early Days of the Industrial Revolution* (London, 1926), 10-19.

The interest in vital statistics fostered the formation of societies for the assurance of lives. The first half of the eighteenth century saw many visionary schemes, and the plans of the early societies were devised by men who had more optimism than information. The sound operation of any insurance plan presupposes knowledge of the rates of mortality and life expectancy. The facts were not available until the time of Price.

His *Observations on Reversionary Payments* . . . , dedicated to the Earl of Shelburne, appeared in 1771.[6] The preface explained that Price became interested in the subject of annuities when three gentlemen consulted him about the soundness of the plan of the Society for Equitable Assurance on Lives and Survivorships. Price, whose work on the doctrine of chances had acquainted him with mortality tables, pronounced the scheme inadequate, and it was discarded. The Equitable Society, which had already been criticized by the law officers of the crown, reorganized as a voluntary society in 1765 and appealed to Price for further assistance.

Price began a thorough study of insurance problems by reading the literature upon these subjects. In 1693 Edmund Halley, the famous astronomer and mathematician, drew up a table of mortality based upon statistics of births and funerals gathered in Breslau from 1687 to 1691. He did this after the English government requested his advice in preparing

[6] The full title is *Observations on Reversionary Payments; on Schemes for providing Annuities for Widows, and for Persons in Old Age; on The Method of Calculating the Values of Assurances on Lives; and on the National Debt. To which are added, Four Essays on Different Subjects in the Doctrine of Life-Annuities and Political Arithmetick. Also an Appendix, Containing a complete Set of Tables; particularly, Four New Tables, shewing the Probabilities of Life in London, Norwich, and Northampton; and the Values of joint Lives.* This is the title of the third edition to which I shall refer, except as otherwise indicated. It is much enlarged over the first edition, since it contains the appendix described in the title given above. Cadell published it. The dates of the editions are 2d, 1772; 3d, 1773; 4th, 2 vols., 1783; 5th, 2 vols. with notes by William Morgan, 1792, 6th, 2 vols. and notes by Morgan, 1803, and 7th, 2 vols. and notes by Morgan, 1812. Price was preparing the 5th edition at the time of his death in 1791. The *Annual Register*, XV (1772), 204-206, reproduced some of Price's tables on mortality, as well as some quotations from the book.

for an issuance of annuities as a form of government security. Inadequate as Halley's table necessarily was, its author recognized the crucial aspects of the problem; that at different ages the rates of mortality vary, and that if an annuity scheme is to be sound, the facts must be known about the expectations of life for all age groups. Other men became interested in ascertaining the probability of life for different age groups and sexes. Abraham de Moivre, a Hugenot refugee in England and internationally famous as a mathematician, published in 1725 a book entitled *Treatise of Annuities on Lives*. Dr. Thomas Simpson published a table from the London bills of mortality. Price was familiar with these works and mentioned them in his book.

Actually, the *Observations* was Price's third publication on the subject. In 1769 his paper on life expectancy appeared in the *Philosophical Transactions* of the Royal Society.[7] It was incorporated, with enlargements, into the *Observations on Reversionary Payments* as the first essay (pp. 167-226) of the third edition. In 1770 Price prepared another paper for the Royal Society, and it too appeared in the *Philosophical Transactions*.[8] While he was working out the problem of this paper, Price's hair is supposed to have turned gray in one night of furious concentration. The culmination of these efforts was the *Observations on Reversionary Payments*. A badly organized book, it contained discussions on such tangential subjects as the national debt[9] and the Sinking Fund,[10] while it treated the material relating to annuities and reversionary payments in a miscellaneous fashion.

The first two chapters consisted of a series of questions and answers about specific annuity plans then in operation or under discussion. In general, these plans were inadequate,

[7] "Observations on the Expectations of Lives, the Increase of Mankind, the Influences of great Towns on Population, and particularly the State of London, with respect to Healthfulness and Number of Inhabitants. In a Letter from Mr. Richard Price, F.R.S. to Benjamin Franklin, Esq. LL.D. and F.R.S.," *Philosophical Transactions*, LIX (1769), 89-125.

[8] "Observations on the proper Method of calculating the Values of Reversions depending on Survivorships," *ibid.*, LX (1770), 268-76.

[9] Preface to the third edition, xx-xxxix.   [10] Chapter III.

"having been formed as fancy has dictated, without any knowledge of the principles on which the values of reversionary annuities ought to be calculated."[11] For fixing the premium each member of a society ought to pay annually in order to provide a dependable annuity for his widow, Price attempted to lay down some general rules. He admitted frankly the necessity for making assumptions when reliable data were lacking. Thus, husbands were ordinarily older than their wives; life expectancy differed among occupational groups; Londoners, "as is well known," did not live as long as "the rest of mankind."[12] Obviously, Price was not establishing precise formulae, but he saw clearly what the problems were, and he attempted valiantly to secure reliable information.

After these two practical chapters and the one on the national debt, Price discussed in Essay I the problem of determining life expectancy. The existing mortality tables provided only approximate figures of life expectancy. After considerable discussion of this problem, including some remarks on the decline of the population of London, Price concluded the essay by wistfully hoping for better records of vital statistics that would "give the precise law according to which human life wastes in its different stages; and thus supply the necessary *data* for computing accurately the values of all *life-annuities* and *reversions*."[13] This statement was rather an explanation of his mistakes than an apology for them.

A knowledge of life expectancy being basic to the calculation of insurance premiums, Price explained in detail his procedure in working out a mortality table. To provide a

---

[11] *Observations on Reversionary Payments* (7th ed.), I, 90. Later the London Annuity Society altered its program and upon examination by Price and his nephew William Morgan in 1790, was found to be so flourishing that they recommended an increase of the annuities. The Laudable Society soon fell into difficulties that forced it to reduce its annuities by 35 per cent while increasing its premiums by 20 per cent. *Ibid.*, 94, 96, 102. Price also gave sound advice to the society of the East India Commanders, and when it dissolved voluntarily it returned to each member the full value of his share. *Ibid.*, 119, 121-22.

[12] *Ibid.* (3d ed.), 3 n.   [13] *Ibid*, 211.

sound method for the calculation of risks by combining data on the probability of life with the known returns on money at compound interest, Price set up several mortality tables. One was based upon returns from London, and another, destined to become much more famous, drew upon the well kept parish registers of Northampton. From 1768 to 1780 the Equitable Society computed its premiums from the London Table of Observations. Then, having learned from experience that the London Table gave probabilities of life too low, the society adopted Price's revised Northampton Table. Price calculated the life expectancy of a newborn baby in Northampton as 28.83 years. Adjustments to allow for migration would reduce the figure to 26.41.[14] After the first appearance of his book on reversionary payments, Price continued to work on the subject of annuities, and using statistics still being collected in Northampton, he drew up another table that covered the range of years between 1735 and 1780.

The Northampton Table was used by the Equitable and other life insurance societies well into the nineteenth century.[15] The British government also used it for the issuance of annuities in 1789. The experience of the Equitable Society proved that the table erred on the side of caution from the point of view of the society, and in later years people blamed Price for losses to the English public brought about by his mistakes. John Finlaison, actuary and principal accountant of the check department of the national debt office, in 1829 in a report on life annuities said that Price's error in calculating the expectancy of life cost the English people affected by it over two million pounds in eleven years. The table, as experience revealed, overestimated the death rate during the younger ages and underestimated it at the older ages. Price did not allow for the large number of unregistered births, and

---

14 *Ibid.*, 259-62.
15 Buer, *Health, Wealth, and Population*, 14; Thomas, *Price*, 58. Henry Higgs (ed.), *Palgrave's Dictionary of Political Economy* (3 vols., new ed., London, 1923), II, 146, says that Price's table, "even at the present day, has not been entirely abandoned."

he could not have possessed accurate figures on migration. The expectancy of life at the time he compiled his table was probably nearer thirty years than the figures he accepted.[16] Some time after the publication of Price's Northampton Table, a compilation was based on actual enumerations carried out under the order of the Bishop of Carlisle in the years 1763, 1780, and 1787. Known as the Carlisle Table, it was the one used by Finlaison, in its form of 1815. During the nineteenth century other tables of mortality came into use with the increase of knowledge in handling data and of information about vital statistics. The lower death rate shown by the later tables does not prove that Price's figures were excessively erroneous for his time, but rather that improvements in medical science actually increased life expectancy. Mortality tables have frequently to be revised in the light of new circumstances.

Price was also interested in the general conclusions that might be drawn from the existing mortality tables for such places as London, Breslau, Northampton, Norwich, and the Vaud in Switzerland. Admitting the scantiness of the data, he moralized. The deadliest diseases among men were "the off-spring of the tenderness, the luxury, and the corruptions introduced by the vices and false refinements of civil society." "The order of nature is wise and kind." "Let us then value more the simplicity and innocence of a life agreeable to nature; and learn to consider nothing as savageness but malevolence, ignorance, and wickedness."[17] Unwittingly, Price validated the cult of the noble savage with statistical tables! Six sets of figures, taken from the Pais de Vaud, a certain country parish in Brandenburg, Holy Cross near Shrewsbury, London, Vienna, and Berlin, showed life expectancy to be greater in the first three, all of them rural areas. If great cities were the graves of mankind, man was his own grave-digger. "Let us then, instead of charging our Maker with our miseries, learn more to accuse and reproach *ourselves*."[18]

---

[16] Buer, *Health, Wealth, and Population,* 13.
[17] *Observations on Reversionary Payments,* 280-81.   [18] *Ibid.,* 366.

What ought to be done? First, said Price, make an accurate inquiry of the "state of population," that is, a census. Then return to the simple life. Halt the dangerous decline of population by promoting agriculture and a back-to-the-soil movement, checking infant mortality, discouraging sybaritic living, prohibiting enclosures of lands, establishing civil liberty, and reducing the national debt. England would be better off with the kind of simple, homely, bucolic society existing in America.[19] Anticipating his good friend Thomas Jefferson, Price desired a nation of small property holders and yeomen farmers.

While preparing his *Observations*, Price became interested in voluntary friendly societies. Working people making small weekly contributions might build up a common fund out of which modest sickness and old age benefits could be paid. Though such societies already existed, many of them were founded upon inadequate plans, and Price undertook to correct some of the prevalent errors. His recommendations encouraged the remarkable increase in the number of box societies, as they were called.[20] It was but a short step to a plan for a national annuity system, and Price took it in company with Francis Maseres. This son of a Huguenot refugee was a talented person who, after an active public career, became in 1773 a baron of the exchequer. He was interested in science, particularly mathematics. He and Price had several friends in common, including Joseph Priestley, Theophilus Lindsey, and Benjamin Franklin. Maseres liked Price's book on annuities. Presently he and Price worked out a scheme for a public system of annuities.

A bill based upon this scheme actually came before Parliament in 1772.[21] It authorized the parish authorities to receive contributions from working people and invest the proceeds in 3 per cent government stock to accumulate at compound in-

19 *Ibid.*, 378-82.

20 Thomas Ruggles, *The History of the Poor* (2 vols., London, 1793), II, 3-5; Frederic Morton Eden, *The State of the Poor* (3 vols., London, 1797), I, 616-17 n.; *Observations on Reversionary Payments* (7th ed.), I, 137-58, for a discussion of these societies.

21 *Journals of the House of Commons*, XXXIV, 33.

terest. Payments were to be made according to tables attached to the act.[22] The plan really provided for old age pensions, with the purposes of giving greater security to the working classes and of lessening the burden of poor relief imposed upon the ratepayers. By emphasizing the latter aspect the supporters of the bill hoped to win the favor of the upper classes.[23] Though Price was not the active proponent of this plan, he furnished the statistical and actuarial information for it. The bill did not pass the House of Lords, and the project for old age pensions was temporarily dropped. This incident, abortive, emphasizes what is often overlooked, that the old mercantilism was not wholly brutal, having within it a strong element of paternalism, and that the laissez-faire conception was not completely to triumph for some time to come.

The appearance of revised and enlarged editions of the *Observations on Reversionary Payments* showed Price's continued interest in life insurance matters. He was preparing the fifth edition when he died. From time to time also he published articles about mortality rates in the *Philosophical Transactions*. One bore the strange title "Farther Proofs of the Insalubrity of Marshy Situations."[24] Joseph Priestley had suggested in a paper to the Royal Society that stagnant waters had noxious effects upon human beings. Price's paper supported this view, while admitting the incompleteness of the data. The *Annual Register* summarized the paper.[25] In the next year Price commented on the disparity in life expectancy between town and country.[26] Dr. Thomas Percival, a Manchester physician, had published statistics indicating a differential between the city of Manchester and the adjoining countryside in favor of the rural area. Price calculated that in

22 *Parliamentary History*, XVII, 640-42.

23 Thomas, *Price*, 59, *Observations on Reversionary Payments* (7th ed.), I, 149-53 n. *Ibid.*, II, 473, contains an allusion by Morgan to this matter, and Morgan then includes (pp. 474-94) a number of tables which Price prepared at the request of a select committee of the House of Commons when it was considering in 1789 a bill for establishing such societies as a measure for the relief of the poor of England.

24 *Philosophical Transactions*, LXIV (1774), part 1, pp. 96-98.

25 XVII (1774), 79-80.

26 *Philosophical Transactions*, LXV (1775), part 1, pp. 424-45.

great cities the ratio of annual deaths was 1:19-23, while in country districts the ratio was about 1:40-50. He got his results from mortality tables for Stockholm, Rome, and London on the urban side, and from Madeira, Vaud, and York on the rural.[27] The reasons for the higher urban rate, Price insisted, were those he had suggested earlier—the luxuriousness and irregularity of town life and the foulness of the city air.

The observant Dr. Percival also commented upon the ratio between male and female births. Price's data revealed it as ·20:19, while Dr. William Derham found it to be 14:13. The female life expectancy was greater, however, because the male led a more hazardous and irregular life, and had "some particular delicacy" of constitution. Eleven years later Price still puzzled over these phenomena. He sent to the Royal Society a paper from Dr. Joseph Clarke of the Dublin Lying-in Hospital.[28] The facts were as Price had stated them in 1775. Dr. Clarke, who had become interested in these matters from reading Price's articles, argued that the male fetus was larger than the female. Therefore it required more nutrition and was more liable to injury at birth. In support of this contention, Clarke's record showed that more women died in giving birth to male than to female babies.

Price's work on all these subjects demonstrated the inadequacy of the statistics upon which life insurance and annuity systems rested. At the same time he and his co-workers collected much new information. Their efforts stimulated and assisted later statisticians, while the facts they recorded possess great descriptive value for the historian.

But Price accomplished good in his own day. Before the third edition of his *Observations on Reversionary Payments* appeared in 1773, several annuity societies were dissolved because their officers learned how inadequate were their plans.[29] Other societies had to be reorganized. These actions spared many confident investors incalculable hardships and disappointments.

27 *Ibid.*, 426-28.   28 *Ibid*, LXXVI (1786), part 1, pp. 349-64.
29 *Observations*, 404.

The contemporary interest in Price's writings upon annuities is evident from the quantity of literature upon the subject that appeared in subsequent years. At least five polemical publications came out within the same decade as Price's book, and well into the next century men such as Finlaison were analyzing Price's work on annuities.

The *Observations on Reversionary Payments* also attracted attention in America. William Maclay entered in his journal for January 15, 1791, "This was a very disagreeable day. I stayed at home and read Price on Annuities. I find he establishes an opinion which I had long entertained that women are longer-lived than men."[30] The book had more significance than might be indicated by someone's testimony that he passed a dreary day reading Price on annuities. The Reverend Charles Chauncy, pastor of the First Church in Boston, read the book in 1772, and praised it. He lent his copy to John Winthrop, a mathematics professor at Harvard, who spoke of it and Price in flattering terms.[31]

Interest in annuity societies existed in the colonies as well as in England. Price's book encouraged a group of New England clergymen and professors to continue with their plans for an annuity society. The Revolutionary War interrupted their work, but in 1785 a bill for the establishment of a society came before the General Court of Massachusetts. In connection with it, Professor Edward Wigglesworth suggested that Joseph Willard, president of Harvard, ask Price

[30] Edgar S. Maclay (ed.), *The Journal of William Maclay* (New York, 1927), 359.

[31] "Price Papers," Massachusetts Historical Society *Proceedings*, 2d ser., XVII (1903), 265. These papers came to the Massachusetts Historical Society in this way: on Price's death, his nephew William Morgan acquired them, using some of them in writing his life of Price, published in 1815; the next person to own them was Morgan's granddaughter, Miss Sara Travers. She left them by her will to her cousin, Miss Caroline E. Williams (author of *A Welsh Family*), a great-grandniece of Price. She gave them to Walter Ashburner, a London barrister and a descendant also of Price's sister, Sally Morgan. Mr. Ashburner presented them to the historical society. *Ibid.*, 262-63. Subsequent references to these papers will be M.H.S.P. (1903).

about the mortality rate among clergy and professors.[32] In his reply to Willard's request, Price approved of the plan.[33] He confirmed Wigglesworth's guesses about the higher life expectancy of clergymen and teachers. He also thought that the interest rate in Massachusetts, 6 per cent as compared with the prevailing 4 per cent in England, assured the safety of the scheme. He suggested following the Swedish tables contained in his *Observations,* which Wigglesworth had already thought of using. On July 27, 1786, Wigglesworth wrote a letter that pleased Price.[34] The General Court had passed the act incorporating "The Massachusetts Congregational Charitable Society," whose plan contained in a substantial way the recommendations of Price. Willard also wrote to thank Price for his good advice.[35]

In the Continental Congress' debates on the commutation of half pay for officers, Price's authority was invoked.[36] It was suggested that the lifetime half pay be commuted into a gross sum payable in installments over a period of years, but it remained to determine the number of years. A subcommittee composed of Hamilton, Madison, and John Rutledge offered a choice between half pay for life or full pay for six years. Hamilton suggested the number "six," being half of the remaining expectation of life as shown by the tables of Dr. Price. In the debate of February 4, 1783, another motion stipulated the number "5½," for this was "the rate taken from Dr. Price's calculation of annuities." Nine states finally accepted a five year commutation. The records of the debates demonstrate that speakers, in referring to Price, assumed their hearers were familiar with the allusions they were making. The tones of the references also show high respect for Price's authority upon annuity problems.

[32] *Ibid.,* 330-34.

[33] M.H.S.P., 3d ser., XLIII (1910), 619-21. Hereafter M.H.S.P. (1910).

[34] M.H.S.P. (1903), 346-47.   [35] *Ibid.,* 347.

[36] *Journals of the Continental Congress, 1774-1789* (34 vols., Washington, 1904-1937), XXV, 863, 865, 889 (January 25, February 4, 1783), Irving Brant, *James Madison: The Nationalist, 1780-1787* (Indianapolis, 1948), 224-26.

In his work on annuities Price warned against unsound insurance schemes, but, he insisted, these were mere "Bubbles" compared to the "Grand National Evil," the growing public debt.[37] "Much has been before said on this subject by writers of more consequence to no purpose; and we shall pursue the paths we are in, till the edge of the precipice towards which we are advancing awakens us, and ruin becomes certain and unavoidable."[38] Continued borrowing without adequate provision for redemption of debt he called "mortgaging posterity, and funding for eternity." Price described the growth of the national debt during each succeeding war of the eighteenth century. In 1773 the alarming total was £138,000,000.[39] Price believed that such a burden would impoverish the nation, destroy the moral fiber of the people, endanger the constitutional system, and discourage the spirit of liberty in England.[40] But there was a preventive for these evils—a Sinking Fund. So simple, so charming, and utilizing the powers of compound interest, it involved nothing more than the "invariable application" of an annual surplus "together with the interest of all sums redeemed by it, to the purpose of discharging the public debts."[41] The Sinking Fund idea became Price's panacea.

Much else in this section of the *Observations* Price repeated in a publication devoted exclusively to the debt problem. In 1772 there appeared his short pamphlet entitled *An Appeal to the Public, on the Subject of the National Debt*. It went through four editions. Once more Price stressed the magic of compound interest and the necessity for keeping a Sinking

[37] *Observations on Reversionary Payments*, xx.   [38] *Ibid.*, xxxix.

[39] There are divergencies in the statistics of public finance during this period due in part to the confused state of the records and in part "to the different methods of compilation adopted." *Parliamentary Paper* [C.-9010], "Memorandum," 1898. E. L. Hargreaves, *The National Debt* (London, 1930), 291, says that the debt in 1763 was £132,000,000, while Price gives it as £146,000,000 and the paper of the National Debt Office [C.-9010], 29, 31, as £128,564,807 in 1763, and £124,963,254 in 1773. While the figures vary, there is agreement that the retirement of the debt in times of peace was slower than its growth in times of war.

[40] *Observations on Reversionary Payments*, 160-61.

[41] *Ibid.* (7th ed.), I, 276.

Fund in continuous operation. Once again he criticized Whig politicians for crippling the fund of 1716, blaming them as much as ambitious militarists for the crushing burden of debt that struck at the "very Being of the State."[42]

Price's writings stimulated interest in the debt question, and within the next few years it became the concern of various pamphleteers. Price's reputation as an expert on public finance spread on both sides of the Atlantic. Chauncy wrote on May 30, 1774, that in his view and the views of others to whom he had shown the *Appeal*, Price had clearly demonstrated how a nation that wanted to could avoid national bankruptcy.[43] The Earl of Shelburne adopted Price's financial doctrines. In 1774 he wrote to Price concerning some unidentified scheme for managing the debt by means of a Sinking Fund arrangement.[44] Whatever it was—and Shelburne and Price concocted many financial schemes—it slept for a decade, to be revived when Shelburne came into office after the fall of Lord North's ministry in 1782.[45]

[42] *Appeal*, 47.   [43] M H.S P. (1903), 266-67.   [44] *Ibid.*, 273.
[45] The Shelburne Papers, particularly Vol. 135, in the William L. Clements Library, Ann Arbor, Michigan, contain some of the jottings of Price on public finance.

CHAPTER VI

FRIENDSHIPS

T HE PRECEDING two chapters might give the impression that Price's turret study was a prison, for he spent long hours in it. But he also got about a good deal. His friends valued his company too much to let him become cloistered, though there was little chance he would. Price was a gregarious person. Besides, he thought he needed daily exercise. He led a busy, well regulated life, but not one governed by unalterable routine.

Price's health, never robust, had improved by the 1770's. He frequently went walking, and rode horseback nearly every day. In somber clothing, a cocked hat, and clerical gaiters, Price's erect little form on the blind white horse was well known in Stoke Newington, Hackney, and in London itself. After the death of his white horse, which occurred about the time physical infirmities forced him to give up riding, he owned no other, though Shelburne offered the pick of his stables. Another part of Price's health program was the taking of cold baths three or four times weekly. Later, sinus trouble made him forego these. Perhaps frequent bathing was the remedy he once prescribed for Benjamin Franklin. In October, 1786, Benjamin Rush wrote to Price that Franklin "has found considerable benefit from the use of the remedy you recommended to him, joined with blackberry jam."[1] This statement suggests an internal prescription, though Samuel Vaughan informed Price only a month after Rush's letter that Franklin was taking long hot baths twice a week.[2]

[1] M.H.S.P. (1903), 354.

[2] *Ibid.*, 355. An internal prescription is also suggested by Price's statement that he sent a book to Franklin containing an account of the remedy.

Mrs. Price, always frail, did not become an invalid until the
·1780's. Occasionally she felt up to the vacation journey to
Wales, and while her husband revelled in the ocean tides,
she, like a good wife, visited with his relatives. Both he and
Mrs. Price looked forward to the annual visits in Wales.
Nevertheless there were times when he preferred not to go
if his wife was unable to accompany him. In September,
1782, they had to miss the family reunion in Bridgend; they
did get to Brighton where Price enjoyed his sea-bathing.
Brighton, an increasingly fashionable resort, was not the kind
a Dissenter would object to. Once Price went there alone for
his vacation, and Samuel Rogers, with a few of his chums,
traveled down just so they could ride back in Price's pleasant
company.

Above all, Price enjoyed meeting with friends and conversing amicably about things and ideas. Through membership in the Royal Society he made the acquaintance of some
of the notable persons of the time, such as Adam Smith, who
became a fellow in 1767. Price remained an active member
of the Royal Society for the twenty years after his election,
and periodically he prepared a paper to be read to the society
and published in its *Philosophical Transactions*. His last contribution appeared in 1786, when he transmitted Dr. Joseph
Clarke's findings concerning mortality among infants. Price's
letters occasionally mentioned the affairs of the society, and
there is also evidence of his attendance at the meetings. On
November 24, 1774, for example, Price and Franklin introduced to the Royal Society a prominent American visitor,
Josiah Quincy, Jr.[3]

The "Honest Whigs" was another organization to which
Price belonged. The club originally met every other Thursday
evening at St. Paul's Coffeehouse, but soon it moved to the
London Coffeehouse on Ludgate Hill. On September 21, 1769,

Price to Rush, July 30, 1786, Rush Manuscripts, The Library Company of
Philadelphia.

[3] "Journal of Josiah Quincy Jr. 1774-1775 in London," M.H.S.P., 3d ser., L
(1917), 443. Hereafter M.H.S.P. (1917).

the ubiquitous and indispensable James Boswell attended this club, "to which I belong," and he described its proceedings.[4] The members were mainly professional men, and their names indicate the prominence of Dissenters in the group. Boswell's account mentioned by name Franklin; William Rose of Chiswick, a schoolteacher; James Burgh, also a schoolteacher, a neighbor parishioner of Price in Stoke Newington, and later the author of the *Political Disquisitions*, a widely read attack upon parliamentary corruption; "Mr. Price who writes on Morals"; Dr. Joseph Jeffries, a "supporter of the Bill of Rights"; and others. These names also suggest the political attitudes of the "Honest Whigs." When the members arrived late in the afternoon, they found wine and punch already on the table. Some of them smoked pipes, and all of them talked, sometimes "sensibly" and sometimes "furiously." At nine o'clock they dined on welsh rarebit and apple-puffs, porter and beer. The cost of the evening's entertainment, noted Boswell, was 18d. for each member.

Among the members Boswell did not mention were Joseph Priestley and Andrew Kippis, both dissenting clergymen; John Hawkesworth, a writer interested in travel accounts; John Stanley, the composer and organist; Peter Collinson, a businessman with scientific interests; William Watson and James Parsons, both physicians and the second a philologian; Mathew Maty and Peter Templeman of the recently established British Museum; and three prominent members of the Royal Society: John Canton, John Fothergill, the Quaker philanthropist, and Sir John Pringle, the president of the society and a well known physician. On November 24, 1774, and again on January 19, 1775, Josiah Quincy, Jr., dined with the group, calling it "a club of friends of Liberty." By this time the quarrel between the thirteen North American colonies and the mother country was a burning topic. Doubtless the talk of the "Honest Whigs"

[4] Geoffrey Scott and Frederick A. Pottle (eds.), *Private Papers of James Boswell from Malahide Castle in the Collection of L't. Col. Ralph Heywood Isham* (18 vols., privately printed, 1928-1934), VIII, 121. Hereafter Boswell, *Private Papers*.

was more largely political than ever before. Certainly the cause of the colonies had stout champions in the group. Quincy found the members hoping that good would come out of the controversy and extending to Americans "the most ardent wishes for their success."[5]

The fame of Samuel Johnson's Literary Club has thrown into obscurity all similar contemporary clubs. Yet the "Honest Whigs" deserve comparison, and I am not convinced that one would not have learned more during an evening with Price's company than he would from hearing the conversation at the Literary Club. For one thing, no Honest Whig domineered as Johnson did; there was greater opportunity for free exchange of opinion than in the Literary Club, which Sir John Hawkins angrily quit because he thought Burke monopolized the talk. If the club talked better on art, literature, and drama, the "Honest Whigs" excelled in science, with such members as Franklin, Pringle, Canton, Priestley, and Price. And where the club had to ban political discussions to keep Burke and Johnson on friendly terms, the "Honest Whigs" throve on politics. Franklin, of course, was the only one whose reputation came to rival Johnson's, Burke's, Garrick's, or Goldsmith's. But if I had to choose between an evening with either of these clubs, I am not certain which I would prefer.

There is no doubt about Franklin's opinion of the "Honest Whigs." On February 6, 1780, he asked Price to pay his respects to the society he had enjoyed so much.[6] He feared he never again would relive the pleasant hours he had spent with "our valuable Club."[7]

The Thursday evening meetings were not the only times when Price met Boswell, or better, when Boswell sought out Price. On Sunday, August 13, 1780, Boswell, low in spirits, turned to religion for comfort. He attended the New English Chapel both forenoon and afternoon, and then he "Looked at

[5] M.H S.P. (1917), 443

[6] John Bigelow (ed.), *The Complete Works of Benjamin Franklin* (10 vols, New York, 1887-1888), VII, 6-7. Hereafter Bigelow, *Franklin*.

[7] Morgan, *Price*, 96 n.

Dr. Price on Providence, etc."[8] Boswell took his religion like
his liquor, not so regularly perhaps, but in large dosages. On
July 6, 1785, he, Price, and others dined at the home of John
Lee, the able and popular barrister. They talked about Pitt
the Younger. Price could speak with authority about Pitt's
financial policy, for he was an unofficial adviser of the prime
minister.[9] Two years later, in another dark mood, Boswell
sought out Dr. Price, but this time he found no solace. Boswell "walked to Hackney and visited Dr. Price. He obliged
me with the rate of an annuity on money sunk. Vexed that I
did not relish his conversation."[10]

Price also belonged in the early 1770's to a Friday evening
club that met in the homes of the members. Price's attendance
at these soirees seems strange, considering the social differences
between him and some of the other members. The conversation centered around literary subjects, and the most notable
member of the set was Mrs. Elizabeth Montagu, the acknowledged leader of the Bluestockings and a literary personage
in her own right. Her anonymous *Essays on Shakespeare* were
highly praised upon their appearance in 1769. Mrs. Montagu,
more nearly than any London lady, established a salon in
the French manner. Johnson, Burke, and Joshua Reynolds
were frequent guests in her home. Here Price met not only
the Earl of Shelburne, but also the esthetic Lord Lyttleton,
who always demanded a seat close to the fire. Lyttleton enjoyed contemporary fame for his *Dialogues of the Dead*
(1760). He thought so highly of Price's religious writings that
he urged him not to waste his talents upon financial and
political questions. Had Price followed this advice, he would
have remained deservedly obscure.

Others who attended the Friday evening sessions were
Thomas Rogers; the Reverend John Burrows; Thomas Mulso,
a lawyer, a man of inherited estate, and later a commissioner

[8] Boswell, *Private Papers*, XIV, 99. The book he mentioned was Price's
Four Dissertations of 1767.
[9] Boswell, *Private Papers*, XVI, 106. See also Chapter XI.
[10] *Ibid*, XVII, 47 (October 12, 1787).

of bankrupts; and his sister, Mrs. Hester Chapone, another widow. Mrs. Chapone was given to honeyed moralizing. In an essay entitled "On Affectation and Simplicity," she described a character named Simplicius, in reality Dr. Price.[11] Although this lengthy sketch is extragavant, it agrees essentially with contemporary judgments of Price.

While the vain man is painfully striving to outshine all the company, and to attract their admiration, by false wit, forced compliments, and studied graces, he must surely be mortified to observe how constantly *Simplicius* engages their attention, respect and complacency, without having once thought of himself as a person of any consequence among them. Simplicius imparts his superior knowledge, when called upon, as easily and naturally as he would tell you what it is o'clock, and with the same readiness and good-will informs the most ignorant, or confers with the most learned. He is as willing to receive information as to give it, and to join the company, as far as he is able, in the most trifling conversation into which they happen to fall, as in the most serious or sublime. If he disputes, it is with as much candour on the most important and interesting, as on the most insignificant subjects, and he is not less patient in hearing than in answering his antagonist. If you talk to him of himself, or his works, he accepts praise, or acknowledges defects, with equal meekness, and it is impossible to suspect him of affectation in either. We are more obliged and gratified by the plain unexaggerated expressions of his regards than the compliments and attention of the most accomplished pattern of high-breeding; because his benevolence and sincerity are so strongly marked in every look, word, and action, that we are convinced his civilities are offered for our sakes, not for his own; and as the natural effects of real kindness, not the studied ornaments of behaviour. Every one is desirous to shew him kindness in return, which we know will be accepted just as it is meant. All are ready to pay him that deference which he does not desire, and

---

[11] "Essay I," *Miscellanies in Prose and Verse* (London, 1787), 20-23.

to give him credit for more than he assumes, or even for more than he possesses. With a person ungraceful, and with manners unpolished by the world, his behaviour is always proper, easy and respectable; as free from constraint and servility in the highest company as from haughtiness and insolence in the lowest. His dignity arises from his humility; and the sweetness, gentleness, and frankness of his manners from the real goodness and rectitude of his heart, which lies open to inspection in all the fearlessness of truth, without any seed of disguise or ornament.

. . . No wonder then that *Simplicity* is so sure of attracting love and approbation, since it implies almost every other virtue.

The American Revolution made it impossible for Mrs. Montagu any longer to agree with such sentiments about Dr. Price, who was now exposed as an incendiary. He ceased attending her salon. His sympathy for those horrid colonists was too much for Mrs. Montagu, who was assured "that the Americans in battle take aim at our officers which makes the service very dangerous"[12]—for people of the upper class.

Price got along much better with people of liberal beliefs. The Abbé Morellet, whom Shelburne met the year before in France, visited England in the summer of 1772. He was a friend of Turgot and the Baron d'Holbach. Like Mirabeau's, the Abbé's hostility to the Old Regime in France stemmed in part from personal experience. He had been confined to the Bastille by a *lettre de cachet* for writing something about Madame de Rebecq which she thought was not flattering. Quite understandably, then, the Abbé advocated legal reforms. He was also a student of political economy, and the freshness of Price's pamphlet on the national debt gave them much to talk about. Price's views on the population question interested the Abbé. When he dined in London with Colonel

[12] Reginald Blunt (ed.), *Mrs. Montagu, "Queen of the Blues"* (2 vols., Boston, 1923), I, 341-42, letter of October 10, 1776.

Barré, Priestley, Price, Franklin, and the Townshend brothers, Alderman James and the Reverend Joseph, the Abbé found "la conversation était bonne, variée, instructive."[13]

Price's relationship with Adam Smith was puzzling. They knew one another well, but Smith's opinion of Price was not clear; he respected Price's judgment on some matters and rather nastily disagreed on others. There is evidence that Smith liked Price, and there is evidence to the contrary. In any case, Smith was not always a pleasant person; his affability on some occasions was matched by rudeness on others. Between 1773 and 1776, Smith worked in London on his *Wealth of Nations.* Franklin later said that Smith "was in the habit of bringing chapter after chapter as he composed it to himself [Franklin], Dr. Price, and others of the literati; then patiently hear their observations and profit by their discussions and criticisms, sometimes submitting to write whole chapters anew, and even to reverse some of his propositions."[14] Smith's conduct at these sessions contrasted pleasantly with his attitude in 1785, during the controversy between Price and William Eden about the population question in England. Smith wrote to Eden that "Price's speculations cannot fail to sink into the neglect that they have always deserved. I have always considered him as a factious citizen, a most superficial philosopher, and by no means an able calculator."[15] Yet four years later when Samuel Rogers visited Scotland, he carried letters from Price and Kippis recommending him to Smith, and these letters "won for Rogers the kindest possible reception."[16] Whatever Smith's

[13] Fitzmaurice, *Shelburne,* II, 234-39, 254-56. Though Price and the Abbé did not correspond, they kept in touch with one another by means of the letters between Shelburne and the Abbé. In 1779 Price's work on the population decline evoked some comment from the Abbé, who detected the fallacy in Price's data. Lord Edmond George Fitzmaurice (ed.), *Lettres de l'Abbé Morellet . . . à Lord Shelburne* (Paris, 1898), 170-72. Frequently, Morellet asked to be remembered to Price. *Ibid.,* 16, 50, 60, 64, 77, 91-92, 105, 111, 135. In this last reference, the Abbé said, "J'aime les *dissenters* et aussi les dissenters politiques." The Abbé declared that Price was one of the men who deserved the most from his country and from humanity. *Ibid.,* 172.

[14] Quoted in John Rae, *Life of Adam Smith* (London, 1895), 264-65.

[15] *Ibid.,* 398.   [16] *Ibid.,* 416.

real feelings for him, Price always spoke kindly of Smith. In 1790 he wrote that Smith's death had affected him considerably.[17] He thought Smith a writer of great ability, and so far as he had ever heard or known, Smith's character was irreproachable.

John Howard, the humanitarian and evangelist of prison reform, "probably had not a more intimate friend in the world than Dr. Price."[18] Formed during their student days at Coward's Academy, the friendship deepened in the 1750's when Howard lived near Price in Stoke Newington. After the death of his second wife, Howard took up the study of prison conditions throughout Europe. During his travels from Ireland to Constantinople and Moscow, he and Price maintained a correspondence. On Howard's stays in England, they saw much of one another. Their intimacy and the respect Howard had for Price's abilities are clearly revealed by the story lying behind the writing of Howard's epoch-making book, *The State of the Prisons* (1777). According to Samuel Rogers, "People are not aware that Dr. Price wrote a portion" of the book.[19] John Aikin, who also had a hand in its preparation, gave the fullest account.[20] Howard took notes during his travels, and when he settled down to writing them out he and an old friend "methodised" them and "copied out the whole matter in correct language. They were then put into the hands of Dr. Price, from whom they underwent a revision, and received occasionally considerable alterations." Howard frankly acknowledged his debt to Price in letters from which Aikin quoted: " 'I am ashamed to think how much I have accumulated your labours, yet I glory in that assistance to which I owe so much credit in the world, and under Providence, success in my endeavours.'—'It is from your kind aid and assistance, my dear friend, that I derive so much of my character and influence. I exult in declaring it, and shall carry a grate-

17 M.H.S.P. (1903), 377.

18 John Aikin, A *View of the Life, Travels and Philanthropic Labours of the Late John Howard, Esq. LL.D. F.R.S.* (Boston, 1794), 16.

19 Rogers, *Table-Talk*, 152.   20 Aikin, *Life of Howard*, 43-44.

ful sense of it to the last hour of my existence.'" It was characteristic of Price not to claim any credit for Howard's book.

Since Howard was a Dissenter and of middle class origin, his relation with Price was not unusual, but Price's intimacy with the Earl of Shelburne, one of the great peers of the realm, an officeholder, and once prime minister, requires explanation. The association was founded on something nobler than similarity of social status, for there could be none in this instance. It was a harmony of intellectual interests and ideas that attracted them to each other. Mrs. Montagu, after meeting Shelburne in 1765, told her husband, "Lord Shelburne seems a young man of excellent parts, great vivacity, desirous of information either by men or books, and I imagine will be a man of considerable consequence."[21] When Price's *Four Dissertations* appeared in 1767, Mrs. Montagu urged Shelburne, who had a taste for theology, to read the book. He did, and he wanted to meet the author; so Mrs. Montagu brought them together at her home. Later Shelburne called on Price. Their friendship rapidly deepened; Shelburne once stated publicly how much it meant to him. Speaking of Chatham, Shelburne said that the "Great Commoner" had not attempted to improve his mind in later years by surrounding himself with men who could teach him, as Shelburne had done with men such as Price and Dunning.[22] This association with Price, however, was not an orgy of brain-picking for Shelburne; it produced mutual intellectual and emotional satisfaction.

After the death of Lady Shelburne in 1771, and after Shelburne's return from his solace on the continent, he and Price were closer than before. Price visited frequently at Shelburne's town house in Berkley Square and at his estate called Bowood in Wiltshire. He helped negotiate the unfortunate appointment of Joseph Priestley as Shelburne's librarian in the summer of 1772.[23] Priestley was preaching at Leeds, and on

[21] Blunt (ed.), *Mrs. Montagu*, I, 127.   [22] Fitzmaurice, *Shelburne*, III, 32.
[23] John Towill Rutt, *Life and Correspondence of Joseph Priestley, LL.D., F.R.S.* (2 vols., London, 1831-1832), I, 175-85, and Fitzmaurice, *Shelburne*, II, 239-43, tell the story.

one of his visits to London Price introduced him to Shelburne, who wished to meet the man of science. Soon afterward he offered the librarianship to Priestley, who really did not want it. Shelburne finally persuaded him to accept. Price was a go-between and adviser to Priestley during the negotiations, suggesting the salary of £250 and the other conditions that Shelburne agreed to. When Josiah Quincy, Jr., sought out Price at once upon coming to London in the autumn of 1774, he expressed a desire to know Shelburne, a friend of the colonies. Price requested an interview, and the introduction took place at the house in Berkley Square promptly at 10 a.m. on December 12.

Shelburne asked Price's advice upon various matters, personal and local, public and national. He did not conceal his admiration for Price's judgment and knowledge. When he became first minister in 1782, Shelburne offered Price the post of private secretary. Price refused, saying Shelburne might just as well make him Master of Horse.[24] Probably this offer was a kindly gesture on Shelburne's part. Nevertheless, Shelburne in Parliament acknowledged his debt to Price's teachings on financial subjects, and during his ministry over the winter of 1782-1783 there was much discussion between them about the finances of the kingdom.[25] Price's nephew and biographer, who was living in London at the time and saw much of his uncle, asserted that his uncle suggested and perhaps wrote the section of the speech from the throne of December, 1782, expressing a wish for economy and for reduction of the national debt.[26] Under Price's tutelage, Shelburne became an advocate of the Sinking Fund. Soon after the signing of the treaty of commerce with France in 1786, he proposed to found a newspaper called the *Neutralist*, devoted to propagating the doctrine of free trade. He asked Price to leave his theological wrangles and dedicate the rest of his life, in company with himself, to promoting peace and opposing wars.[27]

Price's friendships followed a pattern resting largely upon community of intellectual and political interests. Shelburne

24 Fitzmaurice, *Shelburne*, III, 227.   25 See below, Chapter X.
26 Morgan, *Price*, 97.   27 Fitzmaurice, *Shelburne*, III, 439.

LORD SHELBURNE
1st Marquis of Lansdowne, 1737-1805

(by Sir Joshua Reynolds)

was his closest noble friend, though some of Mrs. Montagu's group also belonged to the aristocracy. When Price parted company with the Bluestockings during the American Revolution, it was because his political views, which for the first time he expressed publicly, proved to be objectionable. Mainly he associated with men of the middle class, Dissenters such as Theophilus Lindsey and Thomas Brand-Hollis, or fellows of the Royal Society whose interests in science and kindred subjects he shared.

Dr. Johnson's circle was closed to Price. Here was definitely an instance of religious discrimination. As the revolutionary spirit mounted toward the end of the eighteenth century and the very foundations of the old order of church and state seemed to be endangered, Burke grew more suspicious of Dissenters. He never was intimate with them anyway. Johnson himself had always been a stanch Church of England man and the most unbending of Tories. He refused to give "countenance to men whose writings he considered as pernicious to society." Once at Oxford, according to Boswell who saw the incident, Johnson left the room when Price entered.[28]

The reasons why Price could not be a friend of Johnson were the same reasons why he had so much in common with Americans. Of all he knew or corresponded with, Franklin was his best friend. They met between 1757 and August, 1762, when Franklin left England. Their meeting may have taken place at the Royal Society, for a common interest in science was one of the several ties between them. More likely, since Price was not a member of the society until 1765, they met through some mutual friend. On March 14, 1764, Franklin wrote from America to John Canton, and sent his regards to Price and "the rest of that happy company" with whom he had passed so many pleasant evenings.[29] When he returned to England, the "happy company" was reunited. On March 8, 1766, Joseph Priestley sent to Price one number of his *History of Electricity*,

---

. [28] Clement Shorter (ed.), *Life of Johnson* (8 vols., New York, 1922), VIII, 37, n. 1.

[29] A. H. Smyth (ed.), *The Writings of Benjamin Franklin* (10 vols., New York, 1907), IV, 220. Professor Verner W. Crane of the University of Michigan called my attention to this letter.

along with a note saying that he had written to Franklin a fortnight earlier.[30] Priestley assumed Price had seen the letter, because he directed Franklin to show it to him and Canton, and "Writing upon a philosophical subject to any of you, I would have it considered as writing to you all." Clearly Price and Franklin saw one another frequently. Later in the year these three men introduced Priestley into the Royal Society.

The earliest correspondence between Price and Franklin, apart from the formal exchange of the article on the doctrine of chances, appears to be a letter dated August 1, 1767, from Franklin to Price.[31] It concerned an honorary degree for the Reverend Andrew Eliot of Boston. Franklin intended to apply to the University of Glasgow, providing Price approved and would also send a recommendation. The letter is an interesting sidelight upon the traffic in honorary degrees. Having already applied to the University of Edinburgh for three other persons, Franklin preferred to seek Eliot's degree from Glasgow. Perhaps Price overcame Franklin's scruples about making a fourth request, because later in the year Edinburgh conferred a degree upon Eliot. Price's honorary D.D., already mentioned, came in a similar manner. Some dissenting friends, without Price's knowledge, made the application to Marischal College, Aberdeen, and paid the fee for him.

It is impossible to say precisely what were Franklin's religious beliefs, though he had a deep interest in religion and morals. He attended Price's church. On September 28, 1772, he wrote to Price in behalf of Sir John Pringle, who had asked him to recommend a preacher of "rational Christianity."[32] Franklin suggested attendance at Price's chapel in Newington, and he warned Price to expect their presence the next Sunday. Franklin was not the only American who listened to Price's preaching. While minister to the Court of St. James after the American Revolution, John Adams attended Price's chapel with "entire satisfaction."

In February, 1774, Price, Franklin, Priestley, and several other kindred curious spirits went to Putney Heath, where

---

[30] Rutt, *Priestley*, I, 57 n.   [31] M.H.S.P. (1903), 263-64.   [32] *Ibid.*, 264.

David Hartley the younger was showing his new fireproof home. The inventor of the stove would surely be interested in this "fireproofing" which consisted of iron plates under the floors and ceilings. Each room was sealed off from those adjoining. Perhaps Price extolled Hartley's invention to Mrs. Montagu; at any rate when she built her new home she used this kind of plating.

This minor incident is one of the last recorded meetings of Price and Franklin. Because of the mounting crisis in relations with the colonies, Franklin soon after left England. He and Price never met again, but they remained warm friends through their correspondence.

During the decade of the 1770's when Price was busy with his writings and his friends, he kept in close touch with his kinfolk in Wales, especially with his sister's two sons, William and George Cadogan Morgan. In 1769 William came to London to study medicine. He lived with Price, who gave him financial aid. When the elder William Morgan died in 1772, his son, somewhat reluctantly, agreed to take over the medical practice in Bridgend. He disliked leaving Price, but in a year he rejoiced at finding an excuse to return to London. His sister Kitty had married Jenkin Williams, also a Bridgend physician, and rather than compete with his brother-in-law, William Morgan threw over the practice of medicine and came again to his uncle.

Just at this time the actuary of the Equitable Assurance Company died. Price, as an adviser of the company, used his influence to secure for his nephew the position of actuary, with a salary of £120 a year and a house in Chatham Place where the company had its offices. Morgan's sister Mary became his housekeeper, though she returned to Bridgend when he married in 1781. He rose rapidly in his new profession. As "Actuary" Morgan he remained with the Equitable Society until 1830. His interest in actuarial science and his attainments in the profession were in large part the results of association with his accomplished uncle, whose work he improved upon.

Price's other nephew, George Cadogan Morgan, also came to London in the early 1770's, and his uncle's influence was as strong upon him. George, who lived with Price in Newington, embraced his uncle's Unitarianism. After completing his studies he went to Norwich, where Dissent was strong, as preacher of the Octagon Chapel. Later he, like William, found an opportunity for returning to London.

While his private life was a happy one, the trend of public affairs in the years before the American Revolution made Price despair. The Wilkes episode had quieted down, but the difficulties between England and the colonies were far from resolved. As a Dissenter, Price had another reason to be unhappy. The campaign of 1771-1773 failed to bring relief from existing disabilities under the Restoration legislation. Since the decision of the House of Lords in 1767 in the case of *Harrison* v. *Evans*, Dissent was no longer a crime in England, and Dissenters could not be punished for refusing to serve in offices from which they were already legally excluded. Yet the Corporation Act still excluded Dissenters from municipal offices; the Test Act still prohibited them from holding offices of trust under the crown; and dissenting clergy and schoolteachers had still to subscribe to certain of the Articles of the Established Church. Official prosecution of Dissenters was almost a thing of the past, but mob fanaticism was a potential danger, and the letter of the leniently administered law was hardly in keeping with the true spirit of religious freedom.

Price's firm belief in freedom of thought was the larger reason for his supporting the movement for relief of Dissenters. He held "that nothing is very important except an honest mind; nothing fundamental except righteous practice, and a' sincere desire to know and do the will of God."[33] The state lacked authority to inquire into a man's conscience. Mandatory subscription to the articles of faith of an established church encroached upon the rights of conscience. The busi-

[33] Richard Price, *The Evidence for a future Period of Improvement in the State of Mankind . . .* (London, 1787), 38.

ness of the state was to protect men's persons and property, not to care for their souls. Concerning religion, the state should do no more, and no less, than to guarantee equal protection and freedom to all denominations.[34]

There were in reality two movements for amending the laws affecting religion. The Feathers Tavern Association wanted to abolish the subscription required of the Anglican clergy and university students. This movement directly concerned only Anglicans. Price, however, sympathized with the spirit of freedom animating the petition of relief which the House of Commons rejected in 1772. One result of the effort, however, was the secession from the Anglican clergy of several men of Unitarian tendencies, among them Theophilus Lindsey.

Price was active in the other movement because it aimed at the legal disabilities suffered by Dissenters. They were encouraged by Lord North's remark, during the debates on the Anglican petition, to the effect that he saw no objection to relief for Dissenters since they received no direct benefits from the Established Church. Burke held a similar view. Thinking the times were propitious, the Dissenters decided to act. Price attended the meetings of the dissenting clergy in London, and he joined the committee formed to prepare the application to Parliament. Shelburne, who encouraged the movement, served as an intermediary with Lord Chatham. On March 18, 1772, he wrote to Chatham that Price, whose books Shelburne had sent to him, and other Dissenters would like to talk with Chatham about the repeal of the subscription clause of the Toleration Act. Accompanying this letter was a protest against the clause, written by Price.[35] Chatham liked the writings of Price, which he commended in a letter to him.[36] When the bill came into the Commons, Burke supported it and the ministry was neutral. In 1772 and again the next year the bill passed the Commons and met defeat in the

[34] Richard Price, *Observations on the Importance of the American Revolution* . . . (Boston, 1784), 22-23

[35] Fitzmaurice, *Shelburne*, II, 247-51.

[36] Thomas, *Price*, 65, letter of January 16, 1773.

Lords, with the Lords Spiritual a phalanx against it. Chatham and Shelburne's support counted for little. The fate of the bill in the Lords partly explains Price's undying hostility to the episcopacy.

In 1779 an act of a somewhat different nature passed. It provided that instead of subscribing to the Articles, the dissenting clergy and teachers need only declare their acceptance of the Scriptures and themselves as Christians and Protestants. Price openly opposed this modification of the Toleration Act because even such a modest affirmation was an infringement upon freedom of conscience. Nothing less than total repeal of the subscription clause and of the Test and Corporation Acts would satisfy him. On December 8, 1787, he preached "an excellent sermon" upholding these beliefs to 303 Dissenters gathered for dinner at the London Tavern.[37]

During these years when Price was forming friendships and working for Dissenters' rights, another struggle involving freedom and the rights of the individual was taking form. To Price, with his pronounced views upon civil and religious liberty, the conflict between England and her colonies was one of the most important events in the history of the world.

[37] Lincoln, *English Dissent,* 247.

CHAPTER VII

THE AMERICAN REVOLUTION

WHILE British politicians quarreled with obstreperous colonials, Price enjoyed the reputation he had earned as a moralist, theologian, mathematician, and authority upon life insurance and public finance. That he had not emphasized politics is not to say that he was politically neutral, but only that an overwhelming necessity for entering the political arena had not yet arisen in his life. The 1740's and 1750's saw little agitation for constitutional reforms, and even Dissenters were quiescent. The imperial crisis, however, drew out Price's latent political interests, and the subsequent reform movement sustained them, so that history remembers him best as a writer upon political subjects. This view somewhat distorts the significance of Price's varied achievements, yet it is not wholly unfaithful. Certainly for the last twenty-five years of his life he played a prominent, if unofficial, role in English public affairs.

Price's interest in politics arose in part out of his dissenting background. English Puritanism had always had its political side, and English Dissent, which was Puritanism redefined by Restoration legislation, necessarily continued the tradition. The Dissenter believed in the doctrine of the career open to all talents, yet parliamentary restrictions still hemmed him in. Mere toleration could not become civil and religious freedom until the statute book was made to reflect the slowly growing enlightenment of the English conscience. The Dissenter had to be a political reformer. By definition he had to participate in politics, so far as the law allowed him, in order to win the larger liberty to which he knew he was entitled.

Few Dissenters in England were republicans, but most were democrats of varying degree for whom the concept of the rights of man was the philosophic basis for political action. The tradition of dissenting liberalism went back beyond John Locke, and it drew heavily upon Milton and his contemporaries of the Puritan Revolution. It was a native liberalism, with little of the influence of French *philosophes* apparent. Interest and idealism mated congenially in the dissenting mind: the repeal of restrictive statutes not only would bring practical freedom to the Dissenter but would restore his dignity as an individual by recognizing his rights under the laws of God.

The American Revolution, more than any event Price had yet experienced, involved principles that every Dissenter held dear. Individual freedom, the worth of the human being, and more generally the rights of man had, even before Locke's day, belonged to the dissenting tradition. The root ideas of this eighteenth century revolutionary creed are nowhere more succinctly stated than in the second paragraph of the American Declaration of Independence. The content of these ideas is well known; what needs emphasis is the universality of the philosophy of revolution. The rights involved were human rights, everywhere and eternally valid, according to the revolutionaries. Political frontiers could not contain them, nor any people claim a monoply of them. Americans justified their resistance to British policies on nonnationalistic grounds. The rights they were defending belonged to mankind; therefore, the rights of Englishmen were at stake in the struggle of the American colonists. Price could not be silent and remain true to himself, to Dissent, or to the greater cause, humanity. Even though it meant opposing his own government, he pronounced without hesitation that the rights of man took precedence over the privileges of Englishmen.

For Price, freedom's justification lay not only in history and contemporary politics, but above all in morality. His moral philosophy, expounded more than a decade before the outbreak of the war, emphasized freedom of choice and the autonomy of the individual. This concept was the foundation for his belief that political freedom likewise required self-government, this time of an entire community. As an elaboration of his moral philosophy, Price's political thought differed from that of many of his revolutionary colleagues and had a sounder basis, but in its purely political connotations it showed complete acceptance of the revolutionary creed. His writings were, therefore, the more easily understood by his hosts of readers who were already prepared to applaud or condemn them. They were popular in their own day because of the clarity and vigor with which Price wrote, and because he was already known as a man of varied talents who was now devoting his attention to political pamphleteering. When the revolutionary enthusiasm should wane, however, and the revolutionary philosophy with its social contract and natural rights no longer appeal or convince, Price's political writings would appear as only a part of a great mass of revolutionary literature, exerting influence in its day but having only academic interest to later generations.

Price also was aware of what was involved in the struggle with America, because he was strongly influenced by his friends and correspondents. No one during the years before 1776 could be long in the company of Franklin, Shelburne, Dunning, or Colonel Barré without hearing discussions of the nature of the British Empire, the rights of the colonists, or the powers of king and Parliament in the colonies. Josiah Quincy, Jr., found the members of the Thursday evening club "ardent" well-wishers of the Americans. Wherever he went during his visit in the winter of 1774-1775, the colonial question entered, for his purpose in coming to England had been "to serve his country wherein he may be able" by "conversing with those, either in or out of administration, who may have been led into wrong sentiments of the people of Boston and the Massachusetts-Province in these troublesome times."[1]

Living in London, Price learned of the official attitudes upon the controversy, as well as of the views expressed in Parliament by the opponents of Lord North's ministry. Barré,

[1] M.H.S.P. (1903), 279, Charles Chauncy to Price, September 13, 1774.

Dunning, and Shelburne were all members of Parliament, and Shelburne was once first commissioner of the Board of Trade and Plantations. Shelburne especially had information that he would pass on to Price. In January, 1775, for example, he sent to Price some "notes" on American affairs; a few months later he made available some "office informations" which, "I need not, I am sure, remind you, . . . require certain managements in the use that's made of them least it should be trac'd to the individual who gives them, and who may be liable to suffer very unjustly."[2]

Through personal associations with Americans in London and through his correspondence with various colonials, particularly New Englanders, Price heard the colonial side of the quarrel. The first notice of the imperial controversy in Price's correspondence occurred in a letter of October 5, 1772, from Chauncy.[3] An ardent patriot, his letters breathed a spirit of defiance that probably contributed to the shaping of Price's views about the quarrel, although Price's general political philosophy was formulated independently of the information he gathered in the months preceding the war. In this letter Chauncy enlarged upon the dangers to colonial liberties implicit in British policy. He could see only two alternatives for the colonists if the British government persisted in its errors: slavery or "an exertion to free ourselves from it." After the passage of the Boston Port Bill, Chauncy felt certain that curtailment of American liberties was the objective of the British government.[4] In midsummer of 1774 Chauncy wrote Price about the spirit of unity in America.[5] The other colonies were assisting beleaguered Massachusetts and preparations were under way for the meeting of a colonial congress at Philadelphia. Though Americans would take up arms to defend their liberties, war was not inevitable. If England would guarantee their "rights and privileges," then the colonists would live peaceably and contentedly within the Empire. Chauncy's other letters emphasized this theme, adding the warning that if war came, Americans would fight to the victorious end.

2 *Ibid.*, 274-75, 307.   3 *Ibid.*, 265.   4 *Ibid.*, 267.   5 *Ibid.*, 268-70.

By this time Josiah Quincy, Jr., was on his way to England, bearing the latest news and also a letter to Price from John Winthrop. After thanking Price for his article on the aberration of Venus, which supplemented a paper Winthrop had written, the American scholar turned to a much more urgent matter, the cause of "distressed America." He told of the disturbing consequences of the Intolerable Acts, urging Price to aid Quincy and to "use the influence which his [Price's] high reputation justly gives him, as far as he can with propriety in favor of the oppressed."[6]

What did Price think of the affair by this time? In a long letter to Chauncy, written February 25, 1775, he encouraged the Americans to resist English oppression.[7] Although Shelburne saw little chance of the fall of Lord North's ministry, Price, perhaps wishfully, expected a change within a year or two. If the Americans remained firm, they could expect better treatment from a new ministry. Whatever the course of English politics, the colonists must continue to resist policies leading to enslavement. What the English government had done to the people of New England, it wanted to do also to the people of England. The colonists were fighting the English battle for liberty, and America must preserve her freedom in order to remain a "future asylum" for the friends of freedom. Price ended with an admonition to be firm and confident, for "God is on the side of liberty and justice."

In the late spring of 1775 Francis Dana, a Massachusetts lawyer, visited England. He carried introductions from John Winthrop and from Ezra Stiles, who was then pastor of the Second Congregational Church in Newport, Rhode Island, and after 1778 president of Yale. At the date of writing his letter, April 10, 1775, Winthrop found the normal course of public affairs suspended and an ominous atmosphere prevailing.[8] He intended to publish some extracts, encouraging

---

[6] Ibid., 271-73, letter of September 20, 1774. Winthrop, who was Hollis Professor of Mathematics and Natural Philosophy at Harvard College, held a chair endowed by the wealthy English Dissenter, Thomas Hollis.

[7] Ibid., 279-81.   [8] Ibid , 283-86.

to Americans, from a letter Price had written to him. Stiles, writing on the same day as Winthrop, told a similar story.[9] The breach between England and her colonists would continue to widen. The Puritans of New England would never forget the Quebec Act, which the bishops in the House of Lords, those "enemies to Truth and Liberty," supported. That law, vowed Stiles, established "the Roman Idolatry over two thirds of the territories of the British Empire," thereby exciting "a Jubilee in Hell and throughout [the] Pontificate." He predicted the formation of new governments in the colonies and the establishment of a permanent Congress and continental army.

Price was already relaying information from England to his American friends, and from his American correspondents to the friends of the colonies in England. On April 12, 1775, William Lee wrote to Josiah Quincy, Jr., who died before landing in America, that Price would send him the information he had promised.[10] Dr. Price, said Lee, also learned from Colonel Barré that four regiments were going to New York, two of them to Albany, and the other troops leaving England were to report to General Gage. After receiving these reinforcements, Gage would take the field. The information Price gathered for Quincy was an account of English taxes and excises, which he sent to Quincy in a letter written in April or May.[11] Price said he heard Lord Sandwich recently in Parliament call Americans rabble and poor fighters. He expected events to prove Lord Sandwich wrong. He urged Quincy to continue writing, for "I have friends in both Houses of Parliament who, as you know, are some of the best friends of America; and I wish to be able to give them the best intelligence."

The next letters from America described the outbreak of hostilities. Winthrop gave a detailed and highly partisan account of the much-disputed battles of Lexington and Concord, placing the blame upon the British who, "without any

[9] *Ibid*, 281-83.   [10] M.H.S.P. (1917), 494-95.
[11] M.H.S.P. (1903), 286-88.

provocation," fired upon the minutemen mustered at Lexington "to defend their property."[12] The British "behaved much in the manner of the Cossacks, firing into some houses, whereby some aged people were killed; entring others, and destroying or pillaging whatever they could lay hands on; and some they burnt to the ground." Boston was (June 6) besieged by the American army; two thirds of the inhabitants had deserted the city and so had the Harvard faculty; Chauncy had fled, along with Winthrop, whose home was occupied by British troops. Franklin was safe in Philadelphia, a member of the new Continental Congress. Edward Wigglesworth, a week later, wanted Price to be on the lookout for Isaac Smith, who had gone to England to become a clergyman.[13] He bore the latest news and would receive newspapers from time to time from his father. Price had two accounts of the battle of Bunker Hill, one a brief description by Winthrop, who also enclosed a newspaper story, and the other, containing the "real truth," by Chauncy, then residing at Medfield.[14] The Americans had made an admirable showing; except for a few Tories they were united and determined.

During the summer of 1775 Price learned about the war from various sources. Shelburne, in Limerick, wrote of the interest the Irish displayed in the American uprising; Franklin asked Priestley to tell Price that America was "determined and unanimous"; William Gordon, in September, chronicled events from the time of Bunker Hill to the date of writing.[15] By autumn Price began to think, with Shelburne, that the colonies were lost and that England faced many troubles, both military and economic.

With the war on in earnest, Price had difficulty exchanging letters abroad. In December his letter to Chauncy reached its destination, but its tone was cautious. Price could not be sure into whose hands it might fall.[16] He avoided comments

---

[12] *Ibid.*, 288-91. [13] *Ibid.*, 293-94. [14] *Ibid.*, 291-92, 294-300.
[15] *Ibid.*, 302-306; W. T. Franklin (ed.), *Private Correspondence of Benjamin Franklin* (2 vols., London, 1833), I, 401.
[16] M.H.S.P. (1903), 306-307.

upon politics, simply saying obscurely that he told Mr. D[ana] and Mr. S[mith] the things he wanted them to carry to Chauncy. As for himself, "I continue to think as I allways did."

From the beginning of the controversy between England and her thirteen North American colonies, Price was consistently sympathetic to the American cause. The letters from ardent colonial patriots doubtless strengthened his belief that the policy of the English ministry was dangerous to political liberty in the colonies and at home. Many Englishmen, in and out of Parliament, feared the growing political leadership of the king, because Parliament might become still more subservient. Too many seats went to placemen, royal pensioners, and timeservers willing to do their royal master's bidding and to sacrifice English liberties for tainted secret service money. Demands for reforms and purification of the representative system in England appeared before and during the American Revolution. Several spectacular affairs, notably that in which John Wilkes was the central figure, warned of threats to political freedom. Opponents of the royal policy did not dissociate American needs from English. Victory over the colonists would dangerously strengthen the king. In thinking about America, Price had an eye upon the domestic political scene.

By the end of 1775 Price decided publicly to pronounce upon the wisdom, morality, and dangers of British policy. The preface of his book was dated February 8, 1776. The next day Joseph Priestley wrote to another dissenting clergyman, the Reverend C. Rotherham, "Tomorrow will come out an excellent pamphlet of Dr. Price's. He sent me a copy last night, and I sat up till after one o'clock to read it."[17] The book was *Observations on the Nature of Civil Liberty*.

Priestley's opinion was indicative of the interest Price's work evoked. The reading public bought up the pamphlet as quickly as copies could be produced. On February 13 Priestley sent to Franklin "a most excellent pamphlet by Dr. Price

17 Rutt, *Priestley*, I, 289-90.

OBSERVATIONS

ON THE NATURE OF

CIVIL LIBERTY,

THE PRINCIPLES OF

GOVERNMENT,

AND THE

JUSTICE AND POLICY

OF THE

WAR WITH AMERICA.

To which is added

An APPENDIX and POSTSCRIPT,
containing a STATE of the NATIONAL DEBT, an
Eſtimate of the Money drawn from the Public
by the Taxes, and an Account of the National
Income and Expenditure ſince the laſt War.

Quis furor iſte novus? quo nunc, quo tenditis ——
Heu! miſeri cives? non Hoſtem, inimicaque caſtra,
—— Veſtras Spes uritis. VIRG.

By RICHARD PRICE, D.D. F.R.S.

THE FIFTH EDITION.

L O N D O N:

Printed for T. CADELL, in the STRAND.
M.DCC.LXXVI.
[Price Two Shillings.]

TITLE-PAGE OF "THE MOST FAMOUS BRITISH TRACT ON THE
AMERICAN WAR"

which, if any thing can, will, I hope, make some impression upon this infatuated nation. An edition of a thousand copies has been nearly sold in two days."[18] A week later Horace Walpole noted some of the reactions to the *Observations*.[19] It "made a great sensation. . . . But the part that hurt Administration was the alarm it gave to the proprietors of the funds by laying open the danger to which they were exposed by ruinous measures of the Court. I think this was the first publication on that side that made any impression. All the hireling writers were employed to answer."

Walpole's suggestion that the London financiers worried about the effects of Price's work upon the price of government securities was affirmed in a letter of the Reverend Theophilus Lindsey to Dr. John Jebb on February 17.[20] Lindsey called the pamphlet "a noble one indeed. I will give you one proof of it. It was yesterday signified to the printer that he would be prosecuted by the Director of the Bank, if he proceeded in printing another, and dispensing it. This menace I am told, had intimidated Mr. Cadell; but that Dr. Price was advised without fear, to print as many copies as the public demanded; and there is an intention of printing it in a smaller size, that it may be an easier purchase." What the bank director had in mind is not clear, but he took no legal action. Cadell and Price carried out their plan, and the editions after the fifth were issued at a reduced price, whereby Price sacrificed profits.

After the pamphlet began to circulate, "Dr. Price's name was in everybody's mouth."[21] Writers, some of them paid by the government, in replying to the *Observations* only encouraged people to read it. The fifth edition appeared on March 12, only a month after the original publication. Within a few months more than 60,000 copies had been sold, a reception entitling the *Observations* to rank as a best-seller. In addition

[18] Jared Sparks (ed.), *The Works of Benjamin Franklin* (10 vols., Boston, 1844), VIII, 171.

[19] A. Francis Steuart (ed.), *The Last Journals of Horace Walpole During the Reign of George III from 1771-1783* (2 vols., London, 1910), I, 529-30 (February 20, 1776).

[20] Rutt, *Priestley*, I, 289 n.   [21] Clayden, *Early Life of Samuel Rogers*, 34.

to the fourteen London editions of 1776, the pamphlet was reprinted in Dublin, Edinburgh, Rotterdam (in French), Braun-
schweig (in German), Leyden (in Dutch, two editions),
Philadelphia, New York, Boston, and Charleston. In America
it was also reprinted in the Hartford *Connecticut Courant* and
the Boston *Continental Journal*.[22] Arthur Lee wrote from London to Lieutenant Governor Colden of New York that "People
here begin to feel the matter as very serious, since the publications of Dr. Price and Lord Stair have convinced them that
new taxes must be imposed for supporting this armament,
which it is certain will cost upwards of twelve millions."[23] In
America William Gordon asked Horatio Gates on June 23
whether he had read Price. Ebenezer Hazard was to have
sent the pamphlet to him.[24] Two months later Franklin sent a
copy to Gates, "as you may not have seen Dr. Price's excellent
pamphlet."[25] It may eventually have reached Benedict Arnold
who, on October 10, asked to borrow Gates' copy.[26] John
Trumbull sent the pamphlet to Philip Schuyler.[27] John Adams
sent it to Samuel Chase.[28] The number of copies sold does
not tell how many people read the pamphlet, for it circulated
among friends. It would be interesting to know what the
common people, who were seldom identified in historical
sources, thought of it. Like Tom Paine's *Common Sense*, it
was probably read on the drumheads and in the taverns.

Although London printers busily turned out refutations of
the *Observations*, a considerable response also was favorable
to Price. On March 14, 1776, the Council of the City of
London voted to bestow upon him the highest honor in its

22 Philip Davidson, *Propaganda and the American Revolution, 1763-1783*
(Chapel Hill, 1941), 241.

23 Francis Wharton (ed), *The Revolutionary Diplomatic Correspondence
of the United States* (6 vols., Washington, 1889), II, 83 (April 15, 1776).

24 M.H S.P., LXIII (1929-1930), 323.

25 Wharton (ed.), *Diplomatic Correspondence*, II, 134.

26 Carl Van Doren, *Secret History of the American Revolution* (New York,
1941), 152.

27 Davidson, *Propaganda*, 216, n. 10.

28 C. F. Adams (ed.), *The Works of John Adams* (10 vols., Boston, 1850-
1856), IX, 421.

power to grant, the Freedom of the City, which was presented
in a gold box worth £50. Price, a frequent auditor of the
parliamentary sessions, was often pointed out as a famous
man to curious visitors. One day at the House of Lords the
Duke of Cumberland told Price he had read the pamphlet until
he was nearly blind, whereupon Lord Ashburton said it was
remarkable that the Duke had been blinded by a book that
had opened the eyes of the kingdom.[29]

Price's political philosophy was neither esoteric nor unusual. Broadly speaking, his views were those commonly held
by the liberals of the period in both England and America.
The pre-eminence of the book, in fact, was derived in part
from its exposition of current political ideas in plausible arguments and in a style that carried a strong emotional appeal.
Price's thought conformed to the traditional doctrines of inalienable rights, individual liberty, and the rights of the
people to rise in rebellion, overthrow a government that had
encroached upon their freedom, and erect a new government
in the place of the one destroyed. Price was not interested
in the state of nature, and to him natural rights were identical
with civil rights. He thought of liberty as a power, not a mere
absence of restraint, for to enjoy civil freedom a man must
not only be unrestricted but must have the opportunity to
participate in public affairs. Indeed, the larger sentiment of
the *Observations* resembles that of the Declaration of Independence, for Price and Jefferson drew upon many of the
same sources.

There was another reason why this pamphlet was so much
better than most of those written by men whose principles
of political action were similar to Price's. His political thought
was raised upon a strong foundation of morality and religious
faith, which made it more congenial to devout persons, particularly in New England. As with morality, so it was with
politics. Freedom was based upon its own rights and not upon
utility. The principles of political and civil liberty were
eternal and valid in themselves, and were not dependent

[29] Thomas, *Price*, 76-77. Ashburton was John Dunning at this time.

either upon circumstances or the state. The essence of political freedom, as of moral freedom, was self-determination of the agent. In the first section of the *Observations* Price made the connection between his moral and political philosophy. Liberty, of which there were four parts, was an inherent right of man. Physical liberty was the power of the individual to act as a free agent; moral freedom was the power to follow one's own sense of right and wrong; religious freedom existed when the individual could believe and worship according to the dictates of his own conscience; and civil liberty was the power of civil society to govern itself by laws of its own making. Civil freedom or slavery depended upon the presence or absence of self-government.

The second section of the pamphlet enlarged upon civil liberty. "All civil government . . . [if free] is the creature of the people. It originates with them. It is conducted under their direction; and has in view nothing but their happiness." It sounded utilitarian for Price to call public happiness the object of government, yet the validity of his principles of freedom was established by right, not utility. "In every free state every man is his own Legislator.—All taxes are free-gifts for public services.—All laws are particular provisions or regulations established by COMMON CONSENT for gaining protection and safety.—And all *Magistrates* are Trustees or Deputies for carrying these regulations into execution." Insofar as these principles did not prevail in the colonies, Americans were not free men.

Where geography prevented direct participation in public affairs by all citizens, Price continued, the next best thing was a representative system. The degree of adequacy of the representation was the test of the existence of political liberty. There must be a wide franchise, and though Price did not specify universal manhood suffrage, he implied the desirability of it. He would put up with a House of Lords and a king, provided the people were fairly represented in one branch of the government, the assemblies in the colonies or the House of Commons in England. The ultimate power in the state resided in the people. "Theirs is the only real omnipotence." Parliament must be subordinate to the will of the people, for there could be no authority in the state "superior to that which gives it being, and from which all jurisdiction in it is derived." The doctrine was the familiar one of the sovereignty of the people. From it all else flowed. The revolutions of 1688-1689 in England, of the American colonies, and later, of the French people were theoretically based upon the precept that if the people were sovereign, their collective will must be authoritative, and the right of revolution and the power to place a new government in the stead of the one overthrown logically followed.

The third section of the *Observations,* entitled "Of the Authority of one Country over another," considered the problem of the empire. There was no liberty in a country whose laws were made by a foreign legislature. The power to legislate for another country could not rightfully be derived from conquest, nor could a people lawfully surrender their civil liberty by agreement. Tradition and prescription, no matter how long their duration, did not validate the authority of one country over another, for "The question with all liberal enquirers ought to be, not what jurisdiction over them *Precedents, Statutes,* and *Charters* give, but what reason and equity, and the rights of humanity give." Price had no objection to a federated empire in theory, but like Burke, he saw practical obstacles to such a solution of the imperial problem.

The conflict was as impolitic as it was unjust, Price declared. England and the colonies alike would suffer. In place of the peace and prosperity that formerly prevailed, there must be expected bloodshed, bitterness, a decline of commerce, an increase of the public debt, inflation of the currency, and finally, the probable loss of the colonies anyway. The war was also dishonorable, for how could policies that subverted human freedom be otherwise?

The last section of the *Observations,* "Of the Probability of Succeeding in the War with England," was strongly influenced by the information Price had received from Chauncy, Winthrop, Franklin, and other patriots. People fighting for their liberties were hard to defeat; England's troops were too few; the Americans stood adamant in defense of their rights; and above all, justice, reason, and Divine aid were on the side of the Americans. Perhaps, said Price, Lord Shelburne's conciliatory proposals, even if adopted by the government, were too late. He was right. The Declaration of Independence came only five months later.

Price's *Observations* evoked a pamphlet controversy that surprised its author. The success of his work, measured not in terms of acceptance by all who read it but rather by the astounding circulation it enjoyed and the discussion it provoked, was phenomenal. At least forty pamphlets were published in the two years after the appearance of the *Observations,* either in support of Price's ideas or, more frequently, in refutation.[30] Some of them, such as John Shebbeare's *An Essay on the Origin, Progress and Establishment of National Society . . .* or James Macpherson's *The Rights of Great Britain asserted against the Claims of America . . .* were sponsored by the ministry; others, such as John Wesley's *Some Observations on Liberty,* sprang from indignation at what their authors considered to be erroneous and dangerous political ideas. The replies to Price showed a variety of philosophical content, some being in the Lockian tradition while rejecting Price's democratic version of natural rights, and others being grounded on utilitarianism.[31]

Wesley's pamphlet illustrated the spirit that prevailed among Price's opponents. In his "Journal" for Thursday, April 4, 1776, Wesley wrote, "I began an Answer to that dangerous Tract, Dr. Price's 'Observations upon Liberty;' which, if practised, would overturn all government, and bring in universal

[30] Lists of replies are given in Thomas, *Price,* 179-82, and H. V. S. Ogden, "The Rejection of the Antithesis of Nature and Art in English Political Writings, 1760-1800" (unpublished dissertation, University of Chicago, 1936), 161-63. These lists are in part supplemental to one another, and the number forty results from a collation of the two.

[31] Ogden, "English Political Writings," 65-69.

anarchy."[32] In his pamphlet he admitted that Price possessed "uncommon abilities" and that his tract was "a masterpiece of its kind."[33] More charitable than most of Price's antagonists, he did not impugn Price's motives, believing he "wrote with an upright intention" and for the purpose of serving mankind as well as the British people. Yet the purity of Price's motives did not mitigate the danger of his ideas.

Wesley tried to clarify the issues. Liberty was not at stake. The colonists always enjoyed religious and civil liberties as subjects of the crown, and only after the recent disorders did Parliament interfere with their concerns. Americans really aimed at independence; behind all their lofty verbiage and high principles lay the desire to separate from the imperial connection. Like Burke, who in his *Letter to the Sheriffs of Bristol* (1777) also answered Price, Wesley professed to love civil liberty, but insisted that liberty was never absolute nor self-government complete because people, in order to enjoy essential liberties, must always be subject to a government and its laws. The disagreement between Price and Wesley, however, was more than a matter of degree. Wesley flatly denied Price's assertions that government was a creature of the people; such views led straight to anarchy.

Wesley's stand reflected both official attitudes and the beliefs of most Englishmen of the period, for the North ministry had popularity among the rank and file in the mother country. According to Wesley, Parliament always possessed the right to legislate for the colonies; Americans enjoyed full rights as Englishmen; the colonists were willfully disobedient to lawful authority. There was no justification for their clamor about being ruled by a legislature in which they were not directly represented. After all, nine tenths of the inhabitants of England lived in the same relationship to Parliament. Here was a fundamental divergence between Wesley and Price; the former saw nothing wrong with the unrepresentative character of Parliament.

---

[32] John Emory (ed.), *The Works of the Reverend John Wesley, A.M.* (7 vols., New York, 1850), "Journal," IV, 450

[33] *Ibid.*, "Miscellaneous," VI, 301. The pamphlet is reprinted, pp. 300-21.

Price, a pacific gentleman, disliked public controversy. He did not at first attempt to answer directly any of the arguments advanced against his own. But as he read the replies that came out against his *Observations*, he was dismayed to find that many of his opponents simply had misunderstood his views. So he prepared a supplement to his pamphlet, and it appeared early in 1777 under the title *Additional Observations on the Nature and Value of Civil Liberty*. Besides a reiteration of his earlier statements, this pamphlet contained some new material, indicated by the remainder of the title which ran *Observations on Schemes for raising Money by Public Loans; An Historical Deduction and Analysis of the National Debt; and a brief Account of the Debts and Resources of France*. Price dedicated this work to the lord mayor, aldermen, and Commons of London in appreciation of the honor they had bestowed upon him. He used this book to point out more clearly, now that another year of the war had gone by, the many dangers facing England. Indifference to the importance of liberty and indulgence in luxury, dissipation, and cynicism were weakening the moral fiber of the English people. The corruption of the controlled House of Commons indicated the waning of civic virtue in England. The increase in the size of the standing army and the inordinate length of parliamentary terms, seven years under the act of 1717, threatened liberty. Just as ominous were the extravagances in public expenditure and the growing power of the crown, matters not unrelated.

The greatest cause for alarm was the deterioration of the English economy. Since 1764, Price asserted, doubtless on the basis of the tables furnished to him by Shelburne, England had an unfavorable balance of trade. The national debt had reached an alarming size, £135,943,051 at midsummer, 1775, with an annual charge of £4,440,821.[34] From historical experi-

---

[34] Hargreaves, *The National Debt*, 291, gives a total of £130,451,006 and an annual charge of £4,814,714 for 1776; *Parl. Paper*, 1898, [C.-9010], 33, gives for the funded debt only, in 1775, a figure of £123,463,254 15 4¾.

ence, which he recounted, and the size of the current expenditures, Price judged that the English people at the end of the American war would be burdened with a debt of £ 200,000,000 at the least.[35] In an earlier pamphlet he had elaborated upon the various dangers of a huge national debt. He also recognized another danger, for he anticipated that before England had resolved her troubles with the former colonies she would again be fighting her traditional enemy. The last section of the *Additional Observations,* therefore, analyzed the economic condition of France. She was far from being a weak nation, and Englishmen, remembering only their recent victory of the Seven Years War, must not delude themselves about the impotency of France. The theme of the entire pamphlet was the gloominess of the outlook for England.

Despite his efforts in the first part of the *Additional Observations* to clear up some of the misapprehensions about his views of civil liberty, Price found that he had not succeeded. So in 1778 he republished both the *Observations* and the *Additional Observations* in a volume entitled *Two Tracts on Civil Liberty, The War with America, and the Debts and Finances of the Kingdom; with a general Introduction and Supplement.* In this lengthy introduction Price said he had paid little attention to earlier charges of his subverting civil liberty, since the accusations emanated from ministerial supporters. Lately a writer "of the first character," a man outstanding for his opposition to the ministry, had echoed those charges. The writer was Burke, and the attack on Price had occurred in the *Letter to the Sheriffs of Bristol on the affairs of America* (April, 1777). Although he sympathized with the colonies, Burke scorned Price's theoretical approach to the American problem. Price was perplexed about Burke's attitude. He could see no fundamental divergence in their views on the origin of civil authority. Admitting the difficulty

[35] Price's prediction was conservative. The funded debt in 1783 was £211,363,254 15 4, in 1784 the funded debt was £227,240,597 and the unfunded debt was £13,685,311, while the annual charge was £9,406,406. *Parl. Paper,* 1898, [C.-9010], 33, Hargreaves, *The National Debt,* 72.

of comprehending the precise meaning of some of Burke's statements, Price was in full accord with the idea Burke had expressed in a pamphlet of 1770 entitled *Thoughts on the Causes of the Present Discontents*. Burke had written "that in all disputes between them [the people] and their rulers, the presumption is at least upon a par in favour of the people," and he also spoke of "the governing part of the state" as being "the trustees of power."

One who is familiar with Burke's political thought can realize that his doctrine of trusteeship was more nearly akin to the idea of *noblesse oblige* than to the democratic philosophy of the sovereignty of the people. Price, however, interpreted these statements of Burke in the light of his own predilections. He could not understand how Burke found his ideas so unsettling when Burke himself had spoken so favorably of the people. Price was saying only that the ultimate authority in the state resided in the people. He thought he saw the same idea in Burke's writings. This difference between Price and Burke was not a matter of prominence in 1778. It was a rehearsal for their far more bitter debate over the French Revolution, when the issue of the sovereignty of the people stood out in sharper focus. The later controversy was all the more dramatic because they not only disagreed in thought but stood on opposite sides concerning the events in France.

In his "Introduction" to the *Two Tracts*, Price noticed another man who had recently attacked him. On February 21, 1777, the Archbishop of York, William Markham, in a sermon to the Society for the Propagation of the Gospel in Foreign Parts, objected to Price's loose talk about civil liberty. Price defended himself by complaisantly agreeing with the Archbishop's definition of liberty being government by law. He would, however, qualify this description by specifying that laws must be made by the common consent of the people expressed through their representatives. The Archbishop, alarmed by the prominence of the Dissenters in politics, had also proposed legal restraints for Dissenters similar to those applied to Roman Catholics. Price reminded him of the historical facts of the firm attachment of Dissenters to the Revolution of 1688, to Whig principles, and to the Hanoverian dynasty. In the same intolerant spirit the Archbishop had advocated an episcopacy for America. If this meant a state establishment for all the colonies, it would destroy the large measure of religious freedom in America where there was— and Price spoke admiringly—"A rising empire, extended over an immense continent, without BISHOPS,—without NOBLES, —and without KINGS."

Price offered a further bit of advice. England could not keep the colonies, even if she repealed all her aggressive acts; but it was not too late to arrive at terms that might win the friendship of the Americans. An accommodation had to be attained quickly before they allied with France. At the date of writing his "Introduction," January 19, 1778, Price was confident that an American-French alliance had not been formed. As events proved, it was already too late. Months would have to pass, in an age of slow communication, before negotiations could get well begun, and on February 6, 1778, the American alliance with France was signed, to be ratified by Congress on May 4.

Price's publications had no effect upon the policy of the British ministry. It is doubtful if his pamphlets changed fundamentally the thinking of any individual. Those who praised his writings were persons who inclined toward his ideas, and those who disagreed with him could hardly be expected to alter opinions held during the decade in which the quarrel with America came to a crisis. These remarks would doubtless be as valid had Price's pamphlets appeared before the war began, when the opportunity for reconciliation of differences was perhaps greater. Burke's magnificent orations on "Conciliation" and "Taxation" changed no votes in a hostile Commons. Certainly Price's ideas, more radical than Burke's, were unacceptable to followers of the royal policy. The ministry, however, worried enough about the wide distribution of the pamphlets to undertake a counterattack, for Price's writings did stir the public. Again, the popular agitations did not force changes in governmental policy.

Shortly after the publication of the *Two Tracts*, an incident occurred that helps in any attempt to assess the influence Price's writings had in America. The leaders in Congress, in trying to solve their financial difficulties, enlisted Price's aid. His support of the American cause and his recognized position as an authority upon problems of public finance brought to him a remarkable offer. On October 6, 1778, the Continental Congress passed a motion "that the Hon. Benjamin Franklin, Arthur Lee, and John Adams, esq., or any of them, be ordered forthwith to apply to Dr. Price, and inform him that it is the desire of Congress to consider him as a citizen of the United States, and to receive his assistance in regulating their finances; that if he shall think it expedient to remove with his family to America and afford such assistance, a generous provision shall be made for requiting his services."[36] The vote by individuals was 16 ayes and 9 noes; by states, 6 ayes, 3 noes, and 3 tie votes. The commissioners sent the resolution to Price, offering, if he consented to move to America, to pay his expenses and give him all assistance in their power.[37] Arthur Lee wrote a personal letter to accompany the official one signed by himself, Franklin, and Adams, strongly urging Price to accept.

Price answered both communications on January 18, 1779.[38] He declined the generous invitation, for he was not qualified to perform the task for which Congress had requested his assistance. Besides America could learn all she needed to know from the examples of England and other European nations. A study of their experiences would show how to avoid a huge public debt and would demonstrate the need for a Sinking Fund as a method of debt redemption. Price also had private reasons for rejecting the offer. Many ties bound him to Eng-

---

[36] *Journals of the Continental Congress*, XII, 984-85.
[37] Adams (ed.), *Works of John Adams*, VII, 71.
[38] Wharton (ed), *Diplomatic Correspondence*, II, 222-24, *ibid.*, III, 64-65.

land; he was happy in his study among his books; he was approaching the "evening of life"; and his health was not firm
enough safely to permit his undertaking a strenuous public
employment.

So he refused, though he was gratified by the kind offer.
It, and the plaudits given him both in England and America,
outweighed the abuses heaped upon him for assisting the
cause of liberty. Please convey to Congress, he requested,
my thanks and my good wishes, and say "that Dr. Price feels
the warmest gratitude for the notice taken of him, and that
he looks to the American States, as *now* the hope, and likely
soon to become the refuge of mankind." In his letter to Lee,
Price said that he had tried "to act the part of a good citizen,
and to serve the best of all causes," and for the future he
could wish for nothing better than that "British America may
preserve its liberty, set an example of moderation and mag-
nanimity, and establish such forms of government, as may
render it an *asylum* for the virtuous and oppressed in other
countries."

This event shows the esteem American leaders had for
Price. It suggests the influence his writings must have had
in encouraging American resistance to England and in convincing Americans of the justice of their revolution. There is
no formula by which, in mathematical terms, one can determine how much a book influences public opinion or even,
more specifically, legislative policy. Historians agree that
Tom Paine's *Common Sense* stimulated the growth of a body
of opinion in the colonies favorable to the assertion of independence from England. Yet no historian can say how much.
Price's *Observations* began to circulate in America only shortly
before the writing of the Declaration of Independence, and it
would doubtless be too strong to say that his pamphlet had
more than a slight influence in strengthening the resolves of
the members of Congress. But Americans continued to read
the *Observations* during the months following the Declaration,
and they also read the *Additional Observations*. Certainly
Price's writings encouraged American readers to continue the

struggle once they had committed themselves to a severance of the imperial connection. Price's views were widely known and highly valued. The respect in which he was held for his abilities in various lines of endeavor gave weight to his utterances on civil liberty and the justice of the war.

CHAPTER VIII

ANSWERING CRITICS AT HOME

HAVING done what he could to clarify the issues and explain the principles involved in the struggle between England and her former colonies, Price withdrew from the controversy. He had not intended to engage in a protracted debate. It was beyond his power to influence the outcome of the war; the course of events was settled. Henceforth, he would watch history unfold and hope that everything that happened was for the best.

In the meantime there were private matters to attend to. Despite the difficulty of sending letters in wartime, it was not impossible to keep in touch with correspondents in enemy territory, either directly or through mutual friends. From Philadelphia in the autumn of 1775 Priestley received a letter from Franklin, who asked him to "Tell our dear, good friend Dr. Price, who sometimes has his doubts and despondencies about our firmness, that America is determined and unanimous, a very few tories and placemen excepted, who will probably soon absent themselves."[1] Occasional letters passed between Price and Franklin during the war years, and Franklin read appreciatively the writings of Price favoring the American cause. From Passy in 1780 he acknowledged receipt of a letter written by Price six months earlier.[2] Franklin had heard of some of Price's personal experiences in the recent past, and he warned, "Take care of yourself; your life is a valuable one. Your writings, after all the abuse you and they have met with, begin to make serious impressions on those who at first re-

---

[1] Wharton (ed.), *Diplomatic Correspondence*, II, 60-61.
[2] Bigelow, *Franklin*, VII, 6-7.

jected the counsels you gave; and they will acquire new weight every day, and be in high esteem when the cavils against them are dead and forgotten."

It was true, as Franklin said, that Price's writings had made him famous, earning for him both censure and acclaim. As he wrote to John Winthrop in June, 1777, "I have drawn upon myself a vast deal of abuse." Horace Walpole, who had an eye for such things, observed after the appearance of the *Additional Observations* how "Shebbeare, the pilloried champion of the Court, abused Dr. Price daily in the papers."[3] Walpole remarked also upon the panic among ministers. Lord Sandwich ordered the arrest of an agitator in whose room lay a copy of Price's pamphlet, taken as evidence of a plot.[4] In 1780 the son of Governor Trumbull of Connecticut was suspected of being a spy. Government agents hoped to find evidence of Trumbull's guilt in his correspondence, for Price's name occurred in it. The court could prove nothing.[5] Mrs. Price, of course, worried. Afraid that harm might come to her husband, she had parcels for him delivered to the home of Thomas Rogers, lest the Price household be searched.[6] She intercepted and concealed from her husband several threats against his life. Price's friends also feared for his safety. Franklin told Winthrop about "some apprehensions" on Price's account "from the violence of government, in consequence of his late excellent publications in favor of liberty."[7]

A correspondent to the *Gentleman's Magazine*, protesting against Price's fast-day sermon of 1779, criticized him for bringing politics to the pulpit.[8] St. Paul did not preach on the national debt, lash ministers, or favor colonial rebellions. "Who that sees . . . the ravings of Dr. Price on the toleration of every political corruption and reverie . . . but must think this poor nation as much over-run with sectaries as even the last century in the height of its distractions." This writer forgot about

[3] Steuart (ed.), *Last Journals of Horace Walpole,* II, 16-17.
[4] *Ibid.*, 11-12.   [5] *Ibid.*, 340.   [6] Williams, *A Welsh Family*, 57.
[7] Sparks (ed.), *Works of Benjamin Franklin*, VIII, 214-15.
[8] Vol. XLIX (1779), 301.

the Archbishop of York and the Bishop of London, who also delivered political sermons. The Bishop of London preached against Price on Ash Wednesday, 1779, in the Chapel Royal.

Scurrility and defamation made Price more cautious, without intimidating him. He continued to convey information abroad, and among certain Americans he had a code number, 176. Thus, Edward Bancroft wrote to Silas Deane from London, February 7, 1777, that "The information which 176 [Dr. Price] gave last week to 64 [Franklin] of the capture of Dr. Irving's vessel on the Mosquito coast and its consequences, is not true."[9] Two weeks later another message went from Bancroft to Deane, "176 [Price] has sent a quantity of newspapers; I shall also add by Mr. Sabbati a parcel containing 4 of Dr. Price's pamphlets directed to some of his Friends."[10] Price received some of his information from Shelburne. On September 24, 1777, Shelburne told him of the worries in official circles over disaffection among Canadians and over the general course of the war, cautioning Price not to mention the source of his knowledge.[11] Price, along with Priestley and other Dissenters, also openly gave aid and comfort to American prisoners of war.[12] These activities of Price were courageous and naive, dangerous and probably useless. Some of them bordered on treason, unless there could be no treason when one was fighting for the rights of man.

Price's pamphlets opened for him two international correspondences, one with a Dutch nobleman, the other with the great Frenchman Turgot. Johan Derk van der Capellen was a friend of liberty much criticized in Holland because of his part in certain local political affairs and because of his championship of the Americans in their struggle for freedom. Believing that Price's pamphlets stated so ably the American case, he translated them into Dutch and published two editions. He explained these matters in a letter to Price, asking pardon

[9] "Silas Deane Papers," New York Historical Society *Collections*, I (1886), 486. The brackets are the editor's.

[10] *Ibid.*, 496.   [11] M H.S P. (1903), 312-13.

[12] Lincoln, *English Dissent*, 49.

for taking the liberty of making some condensations.[13] He also requested Price's good offices in establishing a correspondence between him and Franklin, and he asked for the friendship of Price.

Capellen's letter had been written December 14, 1777, but Price did not receive it until a year later. The letter had become misplaced in the London Custom House, and quite by accident a friend of Price saw it and brought it to him. The letter had never been opened. Price replied immediately, explaining the reason for his delay in answering.[14] He expressed gratitude for Capellen's work of translation and pride in his friendship. He was glad that his pamphlets circulated so widely, for "No work ever proceeded more from the heart" than they, and the satisfaction Price had in the knowledge they were doing good compensated for the abuse they had earned him. As the Baron had discussed Dutch politics, Price discussed those of England. His view of the future was gloomy. He took consolation, however, in the knowledge that in one region, America, civil and religious liberty were understood. Price regretted his inability to introduce Capellen to Franklin, because they had ceased writing to each other lately out of regard for their mutual safety.

The correspondence between Price and Capellen continued only for about a year. Their letters concerned mainly contemporary politics. Because of wartime conditions, the interchange of letters was difficult, and Price suspected that the failure to receive one of Capellen's letters was not accidental. On October 26, 1779, he advised Capellen to address his letters to Mr. Morgan at the office of the Equitable Assurance Society, whereby there would be less danger of their "miscarrying."[15] The crisis with Holland that came to a head in 1780 impeded further correspondence. It was not resumed when peace returned, and the Baron died in 1784.

[13] M.H S.P. (1903), 313-19.

[14] W. H. de Beaufort (ed.), *Brieven van en aan Johan Derck van der Capellen van de Poll* (Utrecht, 1879), 96-100, Price to Capellen, January 25, 1779.   [15] *Ibid.*, 107.

. As Capellen read Price's pamphlets and admired them, so did Turgot. He took slight offense because Price, in the first edition of the *Additional Observations,* mentioned Turgot's "want of address" as a reason for his discharge from the service of Louis XVI two years earlier. Turgot told Price of the true causes of his dismissal, and with this letter began a correspondence that continued until Turgot's death in 1781. Price deleted the objectionable phrase from the subsequent editions of the pamphlet.[16] On March 22, 1778, Turgot thanked Price for making the correction and for the gift of the amended book which Franklin had forwarded.[17] He praised the pamphlet and commended its author as "almost the first" to recognize that liberty did not consist only in living under law, regardless of the unjustness of the laws. This letter was a long one, mostly devoted to reflections on the future of the American states, which apparently had won their independence. Price kept this letter a secret until he published it in 1784 in a work dealing also with the prospects of the new nation.

From the outbreak of the Revolutionary War until the Franco-American alliance of 1778, politics and war claimed Price's attention. He never doubted the righteousness of the American cause, and now French aid assured victory for the former colonies. Though Price did not lose interest in events overseas, he could turn his mind to other matters. Something Priestley wrote demanded refutation, and Price took up his pen to answer the challenge. The result was an epistolary exchange upon a philosophical and religious topic. Perhaps Lord North and his colleagues were relieved to learn that Price, instead of criticizing them, was squabbling with a fellow Dissenter.

The debate evoked comment among contemporaries. Clergymen and scholars may have been interested in its content,

[16] Comte de Mirabeau, *Considerations on the order of Cincinnatus . . .* (London, 1785), 153, n. 1.
[17] W. Walker Stephens, *The Life and Writings of Turgot* (London, 1895), 296.

but its most remarkable feature was the spirit in which it was conducted. The pamphlet wars of the eighteenth century, whether fought over politics or religion, frequently led to enmities among the antagonists. Now, to witness two friends —clergymen at that—dispute like true Christians and gentlemen was a noteworthy event. Shortly after the controversy ended, Bishop Horsley wrote to Lord Monboddo that whatever might be the errors of Price and Priestley concerning the doctrine of materialism, there was "no impiety in their hearts."[18]

Price had read the manuscript of Priestley's *Disquisitions relating to Matter and Spirit,* in which Priestley had expounded the doctrines of materialism and philosophical necessity. Ever since the time of St. Augustine, theologians had differed about necessity versus freedom of the will; yet the question was still a theme of many religious arguments during the time of Price and Priestley. Price's comments on the views Priestley expressed in his *Disquisitions* led to a series of exchanges between them that they finally decided to publish. Their joint effort appeared in 1778 under the long title, in the style of the period, *A Free Discussion of the Doctrines of Materialism, and Philosophical Necessity, In a Correspondence between Dr. Price and Dr. Priestley. To Which are added, by Dr. Priestley, An Introduction, Explaining the nature of the Controversy, and Letters to several Writers who have animadverted on his Disquisitions relating to Matter and Spirit, or his Treatise on Necessity.*

To place the *Free Discussion* in its proper setting, it is necessary to understand the nature of Price's friendship with

[18] Historical Manuscripts Commission *Reports,* Sixth Report, 676-77, letter of November 3, 1780. Lord Monboddo, a Scottish nobleman who delighted in conversation upon scientific and literary subjects, was a friend of Price. They corresponded upon astronomy, for example, and sent their books to one another. On September 25, 1783, Price thanked Lord Monboddo, to whom he had sent his book on annuities, for accepting it and for sending to Price his own work, *Antient Metaphysics. Ibid.,* 673, 677. Listed in the catalog of Lord Monboddo's library is the manuscript of his notes on Price's "Political Arithmetic," meaning Price's work either on population or on the national debt. *Ibid.,* 680.

JOSEPH PRIESTLEY, 1733-1804

(by Ellen Sharples)

Priestley. The characters of the men explain why they argued in good temper. Their amity grew out of a community of interests in science, morality, and public affairs. Priestley dedicated his *Harmony of the Gospels* (1777) to Price and to their union "in the pursuit of natural science, and in an attachment to the natural liberties of mankind." Priestley wrote of Price in his *Memoirs:* "For the most amiable simplicity of character equalled only by that of Mr. Lindsey, a truly Christian spirit, disinterested patriotism, and true candour, no man, in my opinion, ever exceeded Dr. Price. His candour will appear the more extraordinary, considering his warm attachments to the theological sentiments which he embraced in very early life. I shall ever reflect upon our friendship as a circumstance highly honourable, as it was a source of peculiar satisfaction to me."[19] After Priestley fled to the United States in 1794 to escape persecution in England for his religious and political views, he continued to cherish the memory of his friend. On at least three occasions he remarked in letters to Lindsey that Price's portrait, along with others, hung in the study of his Pennsylvania home, and "Though dead, they seem to speak, and tend to inspire good sentiments."[20]

In his *Memoirs* Priestley said that he had been introduced to Price about 1766 by a mutual friend, Dr. George Benson, a dissenting clergyman.[21] The meeting took place at a Mr. Brownsword's home in Stoke Newington, where a small literary society of which Price and Benson were members gathered. This group confined itself to religious and theological discussions. Price and Priestley quickly became friends. Price encouraged Priestley to write his *Address to Protestant Dissenters . . .* (1769); he displayed a helpful interest in Priestley's experiments with air and electricity.[22] With his placid temperament, he was a restraining influence upon the impetuous Priestley. Early in 1770 he chose to suppress a

---

[19] Rutt, *Priestley,* I, 86.   [20] *Ibid.,* II, 359, 412, 486.

[21] Dr. Benson died in 1762. Priestley's slip on the date may be accounted for by his writing the *Memoirs* more than twenty years later.

[22] Rutt, *Priestley,* I, 74, 75 n., 78 n., 87-88.

letter sent to him by Priestley in rebuttal to a newspaper item. Priestley had authorized him to use his discretion in the matter. Price opposed publication of the letter because it would "demean" Priestley to "take notice of anything anonymous."[23] When Priestley became Shelburne's librarian, he asked Price's advice about filling the post he was vacating at Leeds. The successor, Mr. Wood, may have been Price's nominee; at any rate, Price and Dr. Kippis had strongly recommended him.[24] After Priestley came down to London he and Price worked together on many projects. They co-operated in the movement for the repeal of the subscription clauses of the Toleration Act. Price read in manuscript and criticized the second volume of Priestley's *Institutes of Natural and Revealed Religion* (1773).

It was natural for Priestley to ask the advice of Price regarding his *Disquisitions relating to Matter and Spirit*. It was typical of Price to be frank, complete, firm, and good natured in his comments upon Priestley's ideas. Admitting their marked differences on theological questions, Priestley affirmed that "our intentions, I believe, are equally upright, our discussion truly amicable, and consequently *truth*, not *victory*, our object." For "He who can have, and truly *enjoy*, the society of such men as Dr. Price, Mr. Lindsey, and Dr. Jebb, cannot envy the condition of princes. Such fellowship is the true balsam of life."

Priestley's introduction to the *Free Discussion* cleared the ground by stating the areas of agreement and disagreement between him and Price. Their object was the promotion of virtue. They refused to explore the problem of the pre-existence of Christ because Price thought enough had already been written on that subject. They believed firmly in the doctrine of rewards and punishments and that on the day of recompense there would be a "general resurrection." As for materialism, Price affirmed the existence of the soul as an immaterial substance capable of perception and thought, but

---

[23] *Ibid*, 105-107.   [24] *Ibid*, 179, 188.

dependent upon the body for the exercise of these powers. Priestley insisted that these intellectual powers dwelt in the body itself and would be inactive, after the decease of the body, until the general resurrection. This was their first major disagreement; the second was over the philosophy of necessity. Where Price insisted upon moral autonomy as the only valid basis for freedom of the will, Priestley believed that men, as agents of God who placed the proper motives before them, would respond in a necessary and mechanical manner once they chose the course of their actions. Like all necessarians, Priestley had trouble in reconciling necessity and free will. Though a mechanical reaction followed only after a free choice, it was still difficult to separate that choice from deterministic influences.

In the discussion on necessity, Price restated his moral philosophy. Agreeing with Priestley that every action must have a cause, he said that self-determination did not imply absence of causation, because the will of the agent was the cause. Causation was moral as well as physical. Priestley held to the mechanistic view that circumstances which dictated actions provided the necessary motives. The necessarian doctrine is never morally satisfying.

The book was verbose and not particularly enlightening. In addition to the text there were letters from Priestley to various persons, and interchanges between Priestley and Price on the subjects already mentioned. The book reviewed adequately the elements of the problem of materialism and necessity, but it added nothing new to arguments advanced by many previous writers. Its main attractions for readers of that time were its unusual plan and the spirit of friendly disagreement that prevailed throughout. The book was significant, not because of its intrinsic merit, but because of what it revealed about Price and the nature of his friendships. Price was frank and ready to disagree with his friends if he thought their views were in error, but never did he make an enemy out of a former friend by being candid. He disliked hypocrisy, and his friends knew that he said what he believed.

Just a year after the publication of the *Free Discussion* Price proved his admiration of Priestley's work and his love of the man. In order that Priestley might continue his scientific experiments, three men agreed to subsidize him for three years, beginning in 1779. William Constable and John Fothergill gave £10 annually each, and Price gave £5.[25]

The debate with Priestley turned out to be only a temporary diversion from matters of state. Violating his announcement that he was done with discussions of public affairs, Price in 1779 re-entered the political arena. More properly, he turned his pulpit into a soapbox. One of his sermons made a particularly strong impression upon his congregation at the Gravel-Pit Meeting House, where he had been morning preacher for the past nine years. Yielding to urgent requests, he published it under the title, *A Sermon, delivered to a Congregation of Protestant Dissenters, at Hackney, on the 10th of February last, Being the Day appointed for a General Fast. With postscript containing remarks on a passage in the Bishop of London's sermon on Ash-Wednesday, 1779.* Another reason prompted Price to publish his sermon. Some of his remarks had been misrepresented, and Price wanted to set straight the record of what he had said.

Though Price's long discourses sometimes put even Dissenters to sleep, this one kept his congregation attentive. The audience had empty stomachs and an interest in politics, and the sermon was strongly political. The text was Gen. 18:32. The dialogue between God and Abraham, described in the context of the verse, showed God as the moral governor of the universe. He not only judged between the good and the evil in Heaven, but also rewarded the virtuous here on earth. The reference to earthly recompense led Price to politics.

The qualities of virtuous men—obedience to law and orderliness in civic conduct—besides saving their souls could save their countries from ruin. But, Price added, law should express the will of the supreme authority in the nation, which was

25 *Ibid* , II, 513 n.

the people; hence, obedience to law meant obedience to one's own will. This was a moral act because it was self-determined. Such seemingly innocent and beneficent morality carried a revolutionary implication. If law should express the will of the sovereign people, and if the good citizen always strove for freedom, then failure to resist tyranny was immoral. Disobedience to law was wrong only when law represented the will of the people. This was getting close to Rousseau's General Will, and also involved logical difficulties.

But this was after all a sermon, and Price's real purpose was to show that virtue rested upon religion. A good man was wholly good, not just a good man in his private and religious life. He was at the same time a good citizen, official, and patriot in his public capacities. Public and private virtue were linked together, and both rested upon religion. Men who possessed this whole virtue were the health and vigor of the state. England had such men, but not often in high office.

The condition of the country proved how bad England's leaders were. Price, a chronic pessimist upon contemporary public affairs, thought England's circumstances as dolorous as at any time in her history. Everywhere one saw vain dissipation and panting pursuit of luxury, crowds flocking into theaters, great losses of life in wars, mounting debts and taxes, and worst of all, the irrational refusal of England's leaders to take advantage of opportunities for improvement. Price feared that England was lost. But good men knew that God would take care of them, no matter what happened to the rest of the world.

This sermon was an important political tract. It clearly showed the most essential element of Price's political thought, that politics was a branch of morals. The criteria of morality were as valid for public conduct as for private.

To the published sermon Price attached a postscript answering the denunciations of him by the Bishop of London in the Chapel Royal. The Bishop branded Price as a seditious person whose principles disturbed public tranquillity. The word sedition was frequently and loosely used in the controversies of the period, and it often meant nothing more than disapproval of opponents' beliefs. Price refused to admit sedition in his utterances. He had always been candid in expressing himself upon political subjects, and his ideas about the rights of men were well known. He never said the English were totally enslaved, but only that a degree of slavery existed as long as Parliament remained unrepresentative and the majority of the people were excluded from political life. He did not invent these ideas, he said; they came from Locke, Montesquieu, and Blackstone. Surely the Bishop did not intend to call them sedition mongers! Then, Price spoke sadly to the Bishop. He admonished him for conduct unworthy of his high estate. He reminded him of the share the episcopacy had, with a few exceptions, in bringing matters to their present pass.

Price had now indicated in his writings what he thought were the major problems and the greatest dangers facing England. During the next four years he issued other pamphlets about these subjects. By the middle 1780's he had reason to believe that his efforts were not in vain. And in the meantime, the affairs of the new nation across the Atlantic, for which he had such high hopes, continued to claim his attention.

CHAPTER IX

THE CONSTITUTION OF THE UNITED STATES

RICE'S relationship to the political course of the United States during the 1780's was hardly less strange or noteworthy than his influence upon England's post-war reconstruction. One difference, however, deserves comment. A Dissenter playing any part in England's public life, and it had to be unofficial because of legal restraints, combated prejudice which dissenting sympathy with American revolutionaries had done nothing to mitigate. In the United States, where his prestige was high and his friendships numerous because of his espousal of the American Revolution, Price's dissenting background added to his stature. Particularly was this true among New Englanders who boasted the same Puritan ancestry as Price. Along with this common heritage of religious individualism, Price shared with many Americans belief in the political philosophy of the Declaration of Independence and confidence in the glorious future of the United States. As much as any of the men who made the revolution, he possessed the vision of the new nation becoming the hope of the world.

But this revelation did not delude him. National greatness did not descend like manna from heaven, though the capacity for it may have been God-given. Soon after the war ended, Price wrote a book about the prospects of the United States. He challenged American leaders to be bold. He urged them resolutely to make changes in their constitutional system and to take the other actions necessary before America could attain the destiny marked out for it. Price's *Observations on*

*the Importance of the American Revolution, and the Means
of Making it a Benefit to the World,* like his pamphlets of
1776 and 1777, was widely read and enthusiastically acclaimed
in the United States. The book and its influence were part of
the story of the making of the Constitution.[1]

As the American Revolution drew to a close, Price's letters
to and from America became more numerous. They concerned
matters intellectual and scientific rather than military and
diplomatic. A letter of July 21, 1781, to Joseph Willard was
typical. Price congratulated his New England friends for
establishing their academy for promoting the arts and sciences.[2]
Fulfilling Willard's request, he sent the incorporation act and
the list of members to the president of the Royal Society,
along with a personal plea that the society encourage the New
England academy. He also delivered Willard's letters to Dr.
Thomas Morrill, the classical scholar, and to Nevil Maskelyne, the Astronomer Royal. He promised Willard a copy
of the fourth edition of his *Observations on Reversionary Payments* when he completed it. He was collecting additional
statistics on population. There were some new scientific de-
velopments that he thought might interest Willard: the *Philosophical Transactions* of the Royal Society contained information upon philosophy and astronomy; the discovery of the
new star Auriga had attracted attention; Priestley was busy
with his experiments on air.

Two events of this period showed the esteem Americans
had for Price. On April 24, 1781, the Yale Corporation voted
to confer the LL.D. degree upon George Washington and
Richard Price.[3] On January 30, 1782, the American Academy
of Arts and Sciences in Boston accepted Price into its fellowship.[4] These honors flattered Price. He sent a copy of the
fourth edition of his *Observations on Reversionary Payments*
(1783) to the academy and wrote a letter of thanks to Wil-

[1] The essence of this chapter is contained in my article, "Richard Price
and the Constitution of the United States," *American Historical Review*, LIII
(1947-1948), 726-47.

[2] M.H S.P. (1910), 610-11.   [3] Thomas, *Price*, 93.   [4] *Ibid.*, 94.

lard.[5] He also sent technical data on Auriga, which was to be named after its discoverer, Herschel. He assured Willard that he had passed on to the two newly elected members of the American Academy, Priestley and Thomas Brand-Hollis, the letters intended for them. In 1787 Price showed his gratitude to Yale. When President Ezra Stiles asked him to purchase in London some scientific apparatus for the college, Price did so, and bore part of the costs.

Throughout the 1780's Price's relationships with his American friends followed this pattern. He exchanged information on new books and scientific activities, conveyed letters and fulfilled requests for various kinds of favors, and made gifts, some of which were solicited, when he felt able. A letter to Benjamin Rush, January 1, 1783, illustrates this statement.[6] In part, the letter was a series of requests. Price asked Rush to circulate some advertisements of a posthumous work of Bishop Hoadly, to supply Dr. Maskelyne with a list of American universities, colleges, and philosophical societies, and to transmit to Dr. Stiles the parcel being sent in care of Rush. He regretted having to tell Rush that he could not set on foot in England a subscription for the support of Dickinson College. Often he had to refuse similar applications from America, though it pained him to do so. In making these refusals, he protected his dissenting friends in the same way that he later saved Priestley from embarrassment. Joseph Willard wanted a donation from Priestley for Harvard College. Upon being asked about it, Price discouraged the solicitation because Priestley could not afford to make a gift. Willard apologized, saying he thought Priestley had made money from his books.[7] He dropped the matter, not wanting to "straiten" Priestley.

Nevertheless, Price did what he could to assist learning in America. In the spring of 1784 he sent Harvard College a copy of his work on annuities and some of the writings of Bishop Hoadly.[8] He donated books to Dartmouth College.

[5] M H.S.P. (1910), 614-16.   [6] Rush Manuscripts.
[7] M.H.S.P. (1903), 339.   [8] Ibid. (1910), 616.

President John Wheelock, on January 25, 1785, conveyed his and the trustees' gratitude, assuring Price that the books would go into the college library.[9] He knew Price would be happy to learn how the college was prospering. Three days later the American Philosophical Society of Philadelphia elected Price to membership.[10] In 1786 President Willard sent Price a catalog of Harvard graduates, a copy of the Massachusetts almanac, an ordination sermon, and the thanks of Harvard for his earlier benefactions.[11] In this year James Bowdoin, governor of Massachusetts and first president of the Boston academy, fulfilled an earlier promise by sending a volume of the *Memoirs* of the New England academy.[12] He also said that the academy would be honored to receive communications from Dr. Price. Could he contribute a paper in time for the next volume of the academy's transactions?

Price remained on such terms as these with his American friends until his death. In July, 1786, he expressed to Willard his interest in some vital statistics from Salem collected by Dr. E. A. Holyoke.[13] In January, 1787, he sent to Willard a copy of his new book of sermons, along with the latest work of Dr. Maskelyne on the expected appearance of a comet.[14] In July, the Reverend William White, first bishop of the Protestant Episcopal Church in Pennsylvania, asked Price to write a letter to the Royal Society in behalf of Joseph Workman, who had a project to lay before it.[15] Benjamin Rush sent to Price, who, he knew, would be interested, a copy of his pamphlet entitled "An enquiry into the effects of public punishments upon criminals and upon society" (1787). The pamphlet had been read to the Society for Promoting Political Enquiries, of which Franklin was president, a copy of the laws of which Rush had sent to Price.[16]

[9] *Ibid.*, 324   [10] Thomas, *Price*, 94   [11] M.H.S.P. (1910), 619-21.
[12] *Ibid.* (1903), 338.   [13] *Ibid.* (1910), 624-25.   [14] *Ibid.*, 625.
[15] *Ibid.* (1903), 370.
[16] *Ibid.*, 366, Nathan G. Goodman, *Benjamin Rush* (Philadelphia, 1934), 384. In a letter of September 24, 1787, Rush Manuscripts, Price spoke favorably of this pamphlet and indicated the similarity between the ideas of Rush and John Howard on penal reform.

Politics, of course, appeared in Price's correspondence with Americans. He watched anxiously during these years for indications of the United States' progress. His letter of January 1, 1783, to Rush spoke of the importance of settling the problem of the federal union. Price disapproved of the existing arrangements; he favored a plan that would give "due energy" to Congress while preserving the rights of the states. "May Heaven grant to the United States the best direction." Six months later he expressed himself more fully.[17]

I feel myself very happy in the approbation of my attempts to serve the cause of liberty which you express in the letter with which you have favour'd me, and which has been deliver'd to me by Mr John Vaughn [sic]. From a regard to the general rights of mankind and a conviction that all dominion of one country over another is usurpation and tyranny, I have allways defended, as far as I have been able, the cause of America and opposed the late wicked war; and in doing this, I have gone thro' much abuse and some danger in this country. The struggle has been glorious on the part of America; and it has now issued just as I wished it to issue; in the emancipation of the American States and the establishm^t of their independence. It is not possible for me to express to you the satisfaction this has given me. I think it one of the most important revolutions that has ever taken place in the world. It makes a new opening in human affairs which may prove an introduction to times of more light and liberty and virtue than have been yet known. This must be the consequence, if the United States can avoid the infection of European vices, and establish forms of governm^t and a plan of political union that shall be perfectly favourable to universal liberty, and prevent future wars among themselves. Should this happen, they will without doubt be the refuge of mankind, and a great part of the world will endeavour to participate in their happiness. I wish I was capable of advising and assisting them. Were I to attempt this what I should recommend, with particular earnestness, would be, a total separation of re-

[17] Price to Rush, June 26, 1783, Rush Manuscripts.

ligion from state policy, and allowing an open field for
improvem^t by a free discussion of all speculative points,
and an *equal* protection, not only of all *christians*, but of
all honest men of all opinions and religions. I see, with the
greatest pleasure, that the new forms of governm^t are in
this respect liable to but few objections.

From what I have said you must conclude that I cannot but be deeply interested in all that is now passing in
America; and that, therefore, it will be highly agreeable
to me to be informed of any transactions there. Any information of this kind will be gratefully received; but I
cannot promise much in return. There is more in this
country to be avoided than imitated by America.

The more Price thought about the matter, however, the
more he convinced himself that he was capable of passing
along some helpful reflections about American affairs. At
any rate, he could be certain, without being vain, that anything he had to say would be heard respectfully by his friends
in high places in America.[18] No one seems to have invited
Price to write a pamphlet of advice to Americans. At the end
of his famous letter of 1778, Turgot had written that America
was still in a period of great difficulties and needed the advice
of enlightened men. He urged Price to be one of those who
should "join their reflections to those of wise Americans. . . .
This would be well worthy of you, Sir; it has been my desire
to excite your zeal."[19] In 1784 Price had not forgotten the
letter of Turgot, but by this time the problem facing America
was a little different. Turgot had been concerned with the
creation of the new state governments; Price worried about
the defect of authority in the general government. Nevertheless, the urging of Turgot may have had some influence
upon Price who eventually did the things Turgot suggested.

[18] Price's reputation in America is suggested in a bit of evidence ex post
facto. In 1788 there was printed in Philadelphia an edition of Price's *Sermons
on the Christian Doctrine*. Among the subscribers were eleven delegates to
the Constitutional Convention of 1787, as well as the wives of two others.
The people in the United States who read Price were also the leaders of
political and intellectual, not to mention social, life.

[19] Stephens, *Turgot*, 303-304.

Price's earliest biographer gives the impression that Benjamin Rush solicited the pamphlet.[20] Morgan erred for two reasons. The letter he cites was written on May 25, 1786, by which time Price's book had already appeared. Moreover, Rush was asking Price to write a pamphlet upon education, and Morgan missed that point altogether. Rush wrote, "I wish to see this idea inculcated by your pen. Call upon the rulers of our country to lay the foundations of their empire in *knowledge* as well as virtue. . . . You must not desert us. . . . A small pamphlet addressed by you to the Congress, and the legislature of each of the States, upon this subject [schools], I am sure would have more weight with our rulers than an hundred publications thrown out by the citizens of this country."[21] Though Morgan was in error about the subject of this letter, the statement of Rush about Price's influence with American leaders was significant.[22]

The chief factor doubtless was Price's own desire to demonstrate his affection by offering his advice, for what it might be worth, to the new nation. On April 6, 1784, he wrote to Franklin, "Indeed I look upon the revolution there [in America] as one of the most important events in the history of the world. . . . I have been lately employing myself in writing *sentiments of caution and advice,* which I mean to convey to them as a last offering of my good-will."[23] He decided to add Turgot's letter as a supplement, but he hesitated because Turgot had written in the margin of that letter a charge of secrecy.[24] Price had the proof run off and sent it to Franklin at Passy with the request that Franklin obtain the permission

[20] Morgan, *Price,* 104-105 n. Price's answer to this letter was written July 30, 1786, Rush Manuscripts.

[21] M H S.P. (1903), 343. See also Goodman, *Rush,* 387, for the title of a pamphlet upon education by Rush, published in 1786.

[22] Similarly, James Sullivan of Massachusetts wrote to Price on October 16, 1786, that the judges of the Supreme Judicial Court "have given *at last* such a construction to our declaration of rights as sets this point [freedom of conscience] upon a liberal and safe footing. I shall not do you justice without observing that I believe your letter did much towards it." M.H.S.P. (1903), 352. I do not know to what letter Sullivan refers.

[23] Bigelow, *Franklin,* VIII, 466.

[24] *Ibid.,* IX, 2-3, Price to Franklin, July 12, 1784.

of Turgot's friends for the publication of the letter. With Turgot dead and the war ended, he saw no reason for maintaining secrecy. Accompanying the proof, he sent an advance copy of the *Observations on the Importance of the American Revolution,* the suggestions in which were "intended entirely" for Americans. On August 2, Franklin wrote that he had performed the mission successfully.[25] About the same time, Price told Joseph Willard of his concern with the state of manners in America, the avarice, the rage for foreign fineries, the luxurious living, and the jealousy among contending groups and the states.[26] He had lately written some advice to America, the pamphlet was nearly printed, and in a few weeks he would send copies to America. "The acceptance of a parcel of them by my friends will be particularly requested." He hoped the goodness of his intentions would gain him a hearing. Before the copies reached America, Franklin was advertising them. He wrote to Benjamin Vaughan on July 26, 1784, that "Dr. Price's pamphlet of advice to America is a good one and will do good."[27]

In a letter to Rush, Price told about his hopes for the pamphlet.[28] Intended as a "last testimony" of his good will to the United States, he wanted a wide circulation for it. He was sending a few copies to Rush who, besides giving two each to Governor John Dickinson and Dr. John Ewing, was to distribute the others at his discretion. John Vaughan and some of Price's friends in Boston would also receive copies for distribution. Price wanted the pamphlet to reach members of Congress. He was printing only a few copies with the idea that if his American friends liked the pamphlet, they would feel free to have it reprinted.

> I think with some pain and anxiety of what I am doing in this instance. I am afraid that some parts of the advice I have given will not be generally liked; but my own mind

[25] Miscellaneous Collection, William L. Clements Library, photostat of original letter in the possession of Mrs. J. W. Williams, St. Andrews, Scotland.
[26] M.H S.P. (1910), 618.   [27] Bigelow, *Franklin,* IX, 13.
[28] Price to Rush, October 14, 1784, Rush Manuscripts.

is deeply impress'd with the conviction of its importance; and my consciousness of having nothing in view but the best interest of the united States (and thro them of the world) leads me to hope that I shall be an object of candour; and that, if, thro' partial views or misinformation, I have fallen into any mistakes I shall be excused. ––I want no apology for Mr *Turgot's* letter. The reflexion on the service I may do the united States by conveying this letter to them relieves me under my apprehensions of the faults that may be found in the other parts of this tract.

The pamphlet did reach members of Congress. Richard Henry Lee, its president, asked John Adams in London to present his compliments to Price and tell him how the members of Congress received their copies "very thankfully and with the respect due to so able a defender of the liberties of Mankind, and the rights of human nature."[29]

The pamphlet appeared in numerous editions. The second London edition came out in 1785, and like the first was distributed primarily in America. In Boston the pamphlet was printed in 1784, and significantly enough, in 1812, 1818, and 1820. It was published also in New Haven, Trenton, Philadelphia, Dublin, and Amsterdam, all in 1785, and in Charleston in 1786. Mirabeau presented an abstract of it, along with comments, in his *Considerations on the order of Cincinnatus.* This work by Mirabeau appeared in French in London in 1784 and 1788, and in English in London in 1785. A Philadelphia edition of Mirabeau's *Reflections on the Observations* appeared in 1786. There can be no doubt of the wide circulation of Price's *Observations.*

How was the pamphlet received? Mirabeau said of it, "This work cannot be too warmly recommended to the Americans. It abounds with judicious observations, sagacious projects, and useful advice; and breathes throughout a spirit of philanthrophy, and a love of freedom."[30] Many Americans had

---

[29] Edmund C. Burnett (ed.), *Letters of Members of the Continental Congress* (8 vols., Washington, 1921-1936), VIII, 174.

[30] Mirabeau, *Considerations*, 107 n.

the same opinion. The Boston *American Herald* for January 3, 1785, contained the following advertisement: "Observe!] 90 Pages in an Octavo Volume for Two shillings, on as interesting Subjects to these [American] United States, as any Thing, perhaps, that has been wrote for a Century past! This day are published, And to be sold by Powars & Willis, in State-Street, Boston, 'Observations on the Importance of the American Revolution; and the Means of making it a Benefit to the World.' By Richard Price."[31] On January 27, 1785, the Boston *Exchange Advertiser* said that Dr. Price's *Observations* "ought not to be passed over with a slight perusal—they ought to be written before every man's eyes, in *letters of gold.* They ought to be imprinted on the mind of every American, and be immediately carried into practice by all the legislatures of the United States. It would perhaps be saying too much to assert that every idea is practicable; but certain it is that most of his remarks are *sacred,* and to us, *interesting truths.*"[32]

There were many testimonies from men who read the work. It would be important to learn what James Madison thought of it. He knew of the pamphlet and probably read it. There seems to be no clue to his opinion about it, though John Randolph, writing to Madison on February 12, 1785, said he thought Price went "too far even for those among us who entertain sentiments the most federal."[33] Jefferson wrote to Price from Paris that he had received a copy.[34] "I have read it with very great pleasure, as have done many others to whom I have communicated it. The spirit which it breathes is as affectionate as the observations themselves are wise and just. I have no doubt it will be printed in America and produce much good there." Americans, continued Jefferson, were becoming aware of the "want of power in the federal head," and the sentiment for enlarging the powers of Congress was

[31] Charles Warren, "Samuel Adams and the Sans Souci Club in 1785," M.H.S.P., 3d ser., LX (1927), 336, n. 23. Brackets in original.

[32] *Ibid.*

[33] Quoted in Brant, *James Madison,* 386. Brant says that Price's book proposed "much less than Madison did."

[34] M.H.S.P. (1903), 325-26, letter of February 1, 1785.

spreading. It was growing stronger partly because Americans began to see that European nations were ready to take advantage of the weakness in American commercial relations. Although Jefferson feared the possibility of trouble among the American states before Congress' powers would be increased, he did not despair. He was sure that any prospects of permanence in the American union would comfort Price.

Six months later, in response to a letter in which Price had expressed anxiety about the reception of his work in America, Jefferson indicated his own reactions about how "it will have been received." South of the Chesapeake there would be few persons who concurred with Price's remarks about slavery. In the Chesapeake region itself, most persons would approve them in theory and a minority in practice, but this minority would include outstanding people. In the northern states most people would applaud because there were very few slaves in that region. What Price said about slavery "will do a great deal of good: and could you still trouble yourself with our welfare, no man is more able to give aid to the labouring side." Among the leading young men of Virginia there was more sentiment for emancipation than in Maryland, and an address to these young men, written "with all that eloquence of which you are master," would be important to any future decision of the question, "perhaps decisive."[35]

Price worried about the reactions to his remarks upon slavery. Writing to John Jay on July 9, 1785, Price recalled that he had sent some copies of the *Observations* to Jay in the preceding autumn.[36] He had learned how some of the leading men of South Carolina took offense at his recommendations about the gradual abolition of slavery and the slave trade. If slavery were to be continued in America, then the revolution, insisted Price, was in vain. The friends of liberty in Europe disliked the paradox of a people who fought to free themselves

[35] Paul Leicester Ford (ed.), *The Works of Thomas Jefferson* (12 vols, New York, 1904), IV, 447-48, Jefferson to Price, August 7, 1785.

[36] Henry P. Johnston (ed.), *The Correspondence and Public Papers of John Jay* (4 vols., New York, 1890), III, 158-59.

in turn imposing slavery upon others. Price repeated these sentiments in a letter to Rush.[37] He was a little hurt by the attitude of South Carolina and wondered if he had not made himself ridiculous by what he had said about the importance of the revolution. Slavery and too great an inequality of property seemed to him inconsistent with the principles of the revolution.

George Washington read the pamphlet soon after its appearance. On January 10, 1785, Richard Henry Lee sent one to Washington, saying he was sure Price would be pleased.[38] Soon after this, Washington requested Benjamin Vaughan to extend thanks for him to "Doctr. Price, for the honble mention he has made of the American General in his excellent observations on the importance of the American revolution addressed 'To the free and United States of America', which I have seen and read with much pleasure."[39] Nearly six months later Washington was still discussing the pamphlet. In June, 1785, Catherine Macaulay Graham and her husband visited Washington, and after their departure Washington wrote to thank Lee for introducing him to such an intelligent lady, whose "sentiments" he was pleased to note "respecting the inadequacy of the powers of Congress, as also those of Doctr. Price's, coincide with my own."[40] The pamphlet was still on his mind as late as November, 1785, when he wrote to thank Price for his book.[41]

G. Washington presents his most respectful compliments to Dr. Price. With much thankfulness he has received, and with the highest gratification he has read, the doctor's excellent observations on the importance of the American

[37] Price to Rush, July 22, 1785, Rush Manuscripts.

[38] James Curtis Ballagh (ed.), *The Letters of Richard Henry Lee* (2 vols., New York, 1914), II, 321.

[39] John C. Fitzpatrick (ed.), *The Writings of George Washington from the Original Manuscript Sources, 1745-1799* (39 vols., Washington, 1931-1944), XXVIII, 62-63.

[40] *Ibid.*, 174 Mrs. Graham was a well known English radical whose views on politics were somewhat more extreme than those of Price.

[41] George Bancroft, *History of the Formation of the Constitution* (6th ed., 2 vols., New York, 1903), I, 466.

revolution, and the means of making it a benefit to the world. Most devoutly is it to be wished that reasoning so sound should take deep root in the minds of the revolutionists. . . . For the honorable notice of me in your address, I pray you to receive my warmest acknowledgments, and the assurances of the sincere esteem and respect which I entertain for you.

John Adams agreed that the powers of the general government should be enlarged. He gently and somewhat ironically suggested that Price went too far in his sentiments about the equality of men. The achievement of such equality was still at an "immense distance."[42] Nevertheless, he considered the gifts of the pamphlet were "valuable presents." Americans could not but be "obliged to you, and any other writers capable of throwing light upon these objects [government and commerce], who will take the pains to give them advice." As for their points of difference, "If you will permit, I should be glad to communicate with you concerning these things."

From New England came additional praise. Jonathan Jackson read the pamphlet and lent his copy to Governor Bowdoin.[43] The governor had read it earlier, for he told Jackson he was pleased with the additions made in the later issue. Jackson, who believed the sentiment for strengthening the general government was increasing, favored a supreme legislature, executive, and judiciary to which the states should surrender authority. William Hazlitt, the father of the famous British essayist, lived in New England at this time. He asked Price to continue his efforts "to meliorate and enlighten this people, and to arouse them to improve and perfect their several forms of government. No man living can influence them so much as you."[44] John Wheelock was not able to tell Price "how great the applause is which its author receives throughout these states."[45]

---

[42] Adams (ed.), *Works of John Adams*, VIII, 232-33, Adams to Price, April 8, 1785.
[43] M.H.S.P. (1903), 327-28, letter to Price, August 8, 1785.
[44] *Ibid.*, 334, Hazlitt to Price, November 15, 1785.
[45] Morgan, *Price*, 107 n.

All of these were private opinions. On the official level there was an important statement. The president of New Hampshire, Meshech Weare, was in February, 1785, too ill to attend the General Court. But he wrote a letter to that body, and in the concluding paragraph he said:[46]

> I have nothing new to lay before you, as I have not received any public dispatches since your last Session. Many things of great importance will come before you. Perhaps the United States were never in a more critical situation, or more depended on the measures that may be adopted, than at this time. Give me leave to recommend to your Perusal, Doctor Price's Observations on the importance of the American Revolution, tho' perhaps you may not fully agree with him in all his Sentiments, there are certainly many things in them, which deserve serious attention. It is my earnest wish, that such measures may be adopted as may issue in the prosperity of this and the United States. I am Gentlemen with every Sentiment of Respect Y[r] ob[t] and Hum[le] Ser[t],
>
> M Weare
>
> Hampton falls
> Feb[y] 1785

Not all of the reactions in America to Price's sentiments were so favorable. In the pamphlet Price had strongly recommended the simple, agrarian life as being congenial to virtue and morality. In Boston during the winter of 1784-1785 there was organized what came to be called "The Sans Souci Club." The members openly flouted puritanical principles by holding dances, playing cards, and performing other similar indecencies. A storm of controversy developed in Boston. Out of the furor came a farce in three acts entitled *Sans Souci, alias Free and Easy*. Price got his dues in Act 3, Scene 1. Mr. Importance called Price's notions "imaginary" and "antiquated." "Modern republicanism is of a very different complexion. . . . The ancient republican spirit is like the old principles of re-

[46] Manuscript State Papers, Revolution, 1784-1786, X, 79. A copy of this document was supplied to me by the New Hampshire Historical Society.

ligion—staunch Calvinism, but now we have modernized them, and united them with the Court stile of taste and fashion." Jemmy Satirist said, "The Doctor's sentiments did well enough in war times, when we were under the influence of Whig principles . . . but now why are we to be dinged with national manners, national debts, economy, industry and such disagreeable subjects?"[47] The tone of these remarks about Price, however uncomplimentary, indicated that he must have been well known to the people of Boston.

These testimonies upon the *Observations* suggest in a general way the extent of Price's influence upon the thinking of American leaders who supported the movement to strengthen the general government. An examination of the contents of the book shows resemblance between the ideas of Price and those of the men who made the Constitution. With this initial similarity, the minds of Americans were prepared to receive Price's views more readily. His book was effective, not because it brought forth a new political philosophy, but because it emphasized ideas already held by Americans. It was important to them to know that a man of Price's prestige approved of their sentiments and was encouraging them to inaugurate constitutional changes.

The revolution, said Price, opened "a new prospect in human affairs, and begins a new era in the history of mankind."[48] Perhaps it was the most important step in human progress since the coming of Christ.[49] During the war the states established liberal governments, which, because the revolution succeeded, would endure. America would become a refuge for the oppressed and the seat of an empire where liberty, virtue, and science would prevail.[50] Anticipating Bancroft, Price saw in all this the hand of Providence.

But more had to be done in order to achieve the fullest measure of virtue and liberty. First, America should redeem

[47] Warren, "Samuel Adams and the Sans Souci Club in 1785," M.H.S.P. (1927), 336-37.

[48] *Observations*, 3. The edition to be cited is the Boston edition of 1784, published by Powars and Willis.

[49] *Ibid.*, 6, 7.   [50] *Ibid.*, 4.

her debts and pay the soldiers, thereby establishing "infant credit" as a nation. Her vast resources, particularly of land, made that task easy. Price rode his hobby by insisting upon the prompt establishment of a Sinking Fund.[51] Americans owed another debt they never could redeem. It was a debt of "Gratitude only" to that general "who has been raised up by Providence to make them free and independent, and whose name must shine among the first in the future annals of the benefactors of mankind."[52] The next problem was the maintenance of peace. External attack was less to be feared than domestic turmoil, and "providing securities against it is their *hardest* work."[53] There must be created a superior power to settle disputes among the states, and to it the states must surrender much. "Without all doubt the powers of Congress must be enlarged."[54] How? Give Congress enlarged power to call out the state militia; allow Congress to exercise a greater financial authority which should not be checked by "the opposition of any minority in the States."[55]

Like most liberals of his day, Price feared an all powerful central government. The changes he wanted must not infringe upon human liberty. Government should not interfere with freedom of discussion or thought; its function was to protect life and property. If "malevolence and bigotry" appeared, government, instead of curtailing freedom, should counteract these evils by encouraging the search for truth. "Nothing reasonable can suffer by discussion," for "The Author of nature has planted in the human mind principles and feelings which will operate in opposition to any theories that may seem to contradict them," and therefore only "overt acts of injustice, violence or defamation, come properly under the cognizance of civil powers."[56] There must be complete freedom in matters of conscience and religion, and not mere toleration. Let re-

---

[51] *Ibid.*, 9-12. Price's ideas on the Sinking Fund were well known in the United States and were seriously considered during the first year of the Federalist regime. Joseph Dorfman, *The Economic Mind in American Civilization, 1606-1865* (2 vols., New York, 1946), I, 288-89.

[52] *Observations*, 13.   [53] *Ibid.*, 14.
[54] *Ibid.*, 15.   [55] *Ibid.*, 16, 17.   [56] *Ibid.*, 18-30.

ligion flourish in the United States, but not as a part of the civil establishment. Let it be a better religion than there was in Europe. Americans must also make provisions for education which should "teach *how* to think, rather than *what* to think." Education should assist in unfolding and developing the young mind. The quest for truth must be undertaken in a humble spirit, for the more one learned the more clearly he realized how little of all knowledge he really possessed.[57] Price's views on education were not unique, but were unusual enough to be refreshing.

Several dangers confronted the United States. The threats of bankruptcy and civil strife could be guarded against by enlarging the powers of Congress. Parenthetically Price preferred a federal structure to a unitary state, and beyond this he scarcely dealt with the machinery of government. Another danger was the growth of inequality of rank and property. As a Dissenter Price believed in the career open to all talent. He feared the emergence of distinctions among men growing out of factors that had nothing to do with inherent abilities. America was fortunate in being neither barbaric nor effete. Let her maintain her rustic simplicity, with a hardy, independent yeomanry the backbone of the body politic. How Jefferson must have approved of this! The state could do something about maintaining equality by prohibiting titles of nobility and hereditary honors and abolishing primogeniture. Let the United States be "a confederation of States, prosperous and happy, without lords—without Bishops—and without Kings."[58]

Still speaking of equality and simplicity, Price had ideas about foreign trade similar to those of another European who

---

[57] *Ibid.*, 43-53. Price also expressed this sentiment to Elkanah Watson, an American who visited him in 1782 After service in the chapel, which, like the congregation, Watson found plain but respectable, Price talked with him in a room behind the pulpit. Watson was impressed by the modesty of Price, who confessed that he had lived long enough to realize how little of the totality of knowledge he possessed. Winslow C. Watson (ed.), *Men and Times of the Revolution: or, Memoirs of Elkanah Watson* (New York, 1856), 141, 148-49.

[58] *Observations*, 60.

gave advice to America, the Abbé de Mably.[59] Foreign trade was beneficial when it promoted the exchange of necessary and useful goods and encouraged international good will. But Americans must guard against becoming dependent upon a luxury trade which would lead to entanglements abroad and the necessity for maintaining a huge navy. Heavy import duties would preserve self-sufficiency. Another bad effect of foreign trade might be the drain of specie from America, followed by the exorbitant issuance of paper money. A well regulated public bank would be useful. Anticipating Washington, Price cried, "Thus singularly happy, why should they seek connexions with *Europe,* and expose themselves to the danger of being involved in its quarrels?—What have they to do with its politics? Is there any thing very important to them which they can draw from thence—except Infection?—"[60] A final word about another danger. "The Negro Trade cannot be censured in language too severe." Price was happy to learn that the United States were "entering into measures for discountenancing it, and for abolishing the odious slavery which it has introduced." Although this must be a gradual process, liberty in America would be incomplete until slavery was abolished. For once, Price pointed to England as having set a beneficial example.[61]

For all his hopes, Price concluded on a note of discouragement. Since beginning this pamphlet he had received accounts that bothered his dissenting conscience. If reports were true that Americans were succumbing to dissipation, luxury, and idleness, if they were losing their simplicity and piety, and if a clashing of interests came to mark the conduct of their public affairs, then the revolution was only the beginning of new misery instead of the dawn of a new era of happiness and progress. Hence the need for bold measures to prevent the dangers he had pointed out from leading to evil consequences.

[59] Gabriel Bonnot de Mably, "Observations sur Le Gouvernement, et Les Lois des Etats-Unis D'Amérique" (1783), *Oeuvres Complètes de L'Abbé de Mably* (19 vols., Toulouse, 1791), XIII.

[60] *Observations,* 63.   [61] *Ibid.,* 68-69.

In 1786 Mirabeau's *Reflections on the Observations* . . . was published in Philadelphia. In general he agreed with Price. Although he thought him unduly apprehensive about some matters, the cautions of the English writer were "dictated by wisdom."[62] He disagreed with Price about public finance, insisting that as soon as the public debt was paid off, America should never under any circumstances incur new debts. He was enthusiastic over Price's view of commerce. Price had shown "a ray of celestial light" on the subject, and Americans should read this chapter of the *Observations* "again and again. Engrave it in your public halls."[63] To Mirabeau as to Price, the pursuit of luxury was inconsonant with the existence of virtue. The inequality of economic status resulting from the growth of commerce would endanger liberty. Mirabeau's book in translation in Philadelphia in 1786 helped keep alive the messages Price carried in his *Observations* of the preceding year.

It is not necessary to relate the chronology of events in the 1780's to emphasize the timeliness of Price's pamphlet. It appeared when sentiment for political change was crystallizing in the minds of American leaders. From the moment of the final ratification of the Articles, some men were dissatisfied with the inadequacy of Congress' powers.[64] The desires for amendment expressed in the private correspondence of some American leaders of the period, the various attempts within Congress to strengthen the Articles, the calling of the Annapolis Convention, and finally, the assembling of the Constitutional Convention, are familiar facts. The point to be noticed here is that Price's pamphlet appeared during the years when men were becoming convinced of the need for constitutional change and were thinking of taking specific action toward that end. How much influence Price's *Observations* had in the growth of the sentiment cannot be ascertained with precision. Some

[62] *Reflections*, 2, 3.   [63] *Ibid.*, 11-12.
[64] Charles Warren, *The Making of the Constitution* (Boston, 1928), part 1; Merrill Jensen, "The Idea of a National Government During the American Revolution," *Political Science Quarterly*, LVIII (1943), 356-79.

things are certain. Anything Price wrote would be heeded by American leaders, his *Observations* was widely read in America, and the views Price expressed were in harmony with the trend of thought during the years 1784-1787. One may say that Price's pamphlet encouraged these American leaders to continue their efforts and helped to convince them that strengthening the general government was wise and necessary.

Price said little about governmental structure. He was more concerned with the functions of government. His earlier writings on civil liberty dealt with the mechanics of government, particularly the problems of representation and the relationship of the legislature to the people. These views were well known in America, and it was unnecessary for Price to repeat them. Yet in the discussions relating to these matters in the Constitutional Convention and in the Virginia ratifying convention, Price was mentioned as an authority and his writings of a decade earlier were quoted. Paradoxically, the man who referred to Price concerning representation was an outstanding opponent of the Constitution as it came to be written. In the debate of June 27, 1787, Luther Martin, speaking of the position of the small states in the national legislature, said, "Price says, that laws made by one man or a set of men, and not by common consent, is slavery—And it is so when applied to states, if you give them an unequal representation."[65] This is the only reference to Price in the records of the convention, but it indicates that the speaker assumed everyone knew of Price. When he set forth his reasons for opposing the Constitution, Martin ranked Price with the greatest political philosophers. In his "Genuine Information" Martin wrote, "a majority of the convention, . . . decided that a kind of government, which a Montesquieu and a Price have declared the best calculated of any to preserve internal liberty, . . . was totally impracticable; and they acted accordingly."[66] George Nicholas in the Virginia ratifying convention "quoted a passage from

[65] Max Farrand (ed.), *The Records of the Federal Convention of 1787* (4 vols., New Haven, 1934), I, 441.
[66] *Ibid.*, III, 197.

the celebrated Dr. Price [Observations on Civil Liberty] who was so strenuous a friend to America, proving that, as long as representation and responsibility existed in any country, liberty could not be endangered."[67] Price could be quoted for and against, like Scripture.

After writing his Observations, Price continued to encourage Americans who were participating in the movement to form a stronger federal. union. On July 30, 1786, he declined the request of Rush to write a pamphlet advocating a system of public education in the United States.[68] He was not in good health, and besides, he had given his best advice on the subject in the Observations. He took "particular pleasure" in the last letter from Rush about the projected Annapolis Convention. What Rush said about "the property, the good sense, and wisdom of America . . . coming forth and taking the direction of public affairs . . . is charming news." Six months later Price spoke again of the political difficulties among the American states.[69] He wrote, "It is a pity that some general controuling power cannot be establish'd of sufficient vigour to decide disputes, to regulate commerce, to prevent wars, and to constitute an union that shall have weight and credit. At present, the power of Congress is, in Europe, an object of derision rather than respect." While the Constitutional Convention was in session, parts of a letter from Price to William Bingham of Philadelphia were reprinted in the Boston Massachusetts Centinel.[70] Among the extracts were statements of Price's concern about the affairs of America and the need for giving to the federal government "DUE STRENGTH AND ENERGY."

[67] Jonathan Elliott (ed.), The Debates in the Several State Conventions on the Adoption of the Federal Constitution (2d ed., 5 vols, Philadelphia, 1907), III, 20-21.

[68] Rush Manuscripts. This is the proposal Morgan mistook for a suggestion that Price write a pamphlet on politics.

[69] Ibid., letter of January 26, 1787. This letter got back to England and was printed in the Gentleman's Magazine, LVII (1787), part 2, p. 631, in the section entitled "American News."

[70] June 30, 1787. Professor Merrill Jensen of the University of Wisconsin provided this reference.

At last Price heard good news. He wrote to Rush on September 24, 1787, of his delight over the assembling of the convention.[71] He was "happy to find that the collected wisdom and weight of so many of the first men in America are now applied" to the task of the "just formation of the federal governm^t." When he learned of the completion of the Constitution, and its provisions, he wrote to Franklin of his happiness.[72] He was more interested in the spirit that would inform the operation of the government than he was in the actual mechanics of the constitutional system. He was gratified to learn of the separation between religion and civil policy, and that freedom of speech, religion, and the press would prevail.

As with his writings on the American Revolution, it would be difficult to deny that Price's words had weight in America. His pleas in behalf of a stronger federal union can hardly have gone unheeded. Many American leaders testified how carefully they attended what he wrote. It cannot be said that the sections of the Constitution that were in harmony with Price's desires were framed according to his suggestions or out of deference to his wishes. The Constitutional Convention would have assembled and the Constitution have been written had there never lived a Dr. Price. Yet the convention and the Constitution it wrote were the products of many forces operating concurrently, and among them ought to be reckoned the books, the letters, and the blessings of Richard Price.

[71] Rush Manuscripts.
[72] Bigelow, *Franklin*, X, 42-44, letter of December, 1788.

CHAPTER X

GLOOM YIELDS TO HOPE

IN THE closing years of the American Revolution, England's fortunes sank low. Spain allied with France in 1779, and in the next year the formation of the League of Armed Neutrality among several northern European nations left England without a friend. Next door, Ireland seethed. At home, discontent was aggravated by apprehensions for England's future. After 1780, the ministry of Lord North faced a restless parliamentary opposition. Dunning, a friend of Price, introduced in April, 1780, his famous resolution "that the influence of the Crown has increased, is increasing, and ought to be diminished," which passed in Commons by a vote of 233-215. From that moment the Whigs began to hope, and after the surrender of Cornwallis destroyed all chances of British victory over the Americans, Whig influence increased amidst a revival of public interest in prospects of a ministerial change and then of reforms. These two subjects were related. The overthrow of Lord North would prove that the royal policy had failed and also clear the way for England's revival. In February, 1782, Fox's motion of censure against the conduct of naval operations lost by a narrow margin, 183-205. Lord George Germain resigned after a cabinet disagreement, and before March ended Lord North announced "that His Majesty's ministers were no more."

The opposition had always branded the king's policy a threat to English liberties and held it responsible for the troubles of England. There was no guarantee, however, that a new ministry could solve the problems or alleviate the burdens of England and her people. To make a satisfactory peace settlement and then to recover England's prestige were large orders. Yet the ministry that accomplished these tasks would have only begun the work of reconstruction. National finances would have to be untangled and the war-swollen debt reduced. A program of political reforms was in order, and to satisfy extremists and moderates alike required skillful management of men. Those who overthrew Lord North agreed generally about the need for purification of the administration through the elimination of wastage and sinecure posts. Not all who wanted these purges favored reform of Parliament. The sobering effect of responsibility might make of once bold critics timorous ministers. If the new ministry were not courageous and tactful, the recovery of England might be long delayed.

As he fretted in his turret study or talked gloomily with his friends, Price concluded that the future was dark, though not quite hopeless. He thought he knew what proper measures ought to be adopted so that England would again be strong, virtuous, and prosperous. Sybaritic living and the prevalence of dissipation were symptoms of the evils of the times. They were also contributory factors. Price firmly believed that the population of England was declining, and this, he said, was the supreme test of the seriousness of England's plight. His test was fallacious. Price exaggerated England's troubles and underestimated her powers of recovery.

For more than a decade Price had worried about the decrease of population. As early as 1765 he was studying the returns of the window-tax surveyors, which tabulated the number of dwellings in England and Wales.[1] Later he used these for his calculations on the population. He mentioned the subject in his *Reversionary Payments* (1771) and returned to it a year later in his pamphlet on the national debt. He also showed that the population problem affected the questions

[1] The Shelburne Papers contain a volume, 117, entitled "Revenue Notes & Calculations by Dr. Price," in which are several papers by Price relating to window-tax returns.

of debts and taxes, and so he was not talking about a merely academic matter. Price's writings awakened some interest. John Wesley's intellectual curiosity led him to make some observations about population during his endless travels. His conclusions differed from those of Price. On Monday, September 9, 1776, Wesley wrote in his "Journal," "Dr. Price says (doubtless to encourage our good friends, the French and Spaniards)" that supposing an average of four or four and a half persons per house, the population was between four and five millions.[2] Wesley set the average at six persons per house.

The variation between these two estimates illustrated the fatal defect in every calculation about population in this period. Nobody possessed accurate national statistics. Every numerical assertion was at best an approximation. A famous early calculation by Gregory King, in 1696, gave a total of 5,500,000 for England and Wales. In 1770 Arthur Young thought the population was 8,500,000. The census of 1801 returned 8,872,980 persons actually counted, or about 9,000,000 if one allows for omissions by unskilled census takers. By working backward from known figures, statisticians have arrived at estimates for the previous decades of the eighteenth century. These estimates differ in numbers, but they show definitely that the trend was upwards, rising from about 6,000,000 in 1700 to just over 7,000,000 in 1770, and to about 7,500,000 in 1780.[3] Price's figure for 1779 was 4,763,000.[4] Though Price's opponents had no better information than he, they were nearer the mark and they are supported by the statistical consensus that England's population increased during the eighteenth century. On the whole, they had the better of the argument with Price.

[2] Emory (ed.), *Works of John Wesley*, IV, 462.

[3] F. C. Dietz, *An Economic History of England* (New York, 1942), 281 Dietz's table varies slightly from that given in the *Encyclopedia of the Social Sciences*, VI, 243. E. C K Gonner, "The Population of England in the Eighteenth Century," *Journal of the Royal Statistical Society*, LXXVI (1912-1913), 261-96, reviews this controversy. Gonner gives a figure of 7,000,000 in 1780.

[4] Buer, *Health, Wealth, and Population*, 12.

Since no one before 1801 could speak with finality, writers accepted whatever estimate seemed best to suit their purposes. Price, like others, used population figures to support political and social theories. He also allowed his social philosophy to color his interpretations of data, and thereby he led others into errors. James Burgh, speaking in his *Political Disquisitions* of the inadequacy of the representation in Parliament, used the figures of "my incomparable friend Dr. Price."[5] Though Dr. Johnson hated Price, he accepted Price's conclusions about the size of the population. On April 20, 1783, before the pamphlet controversy touched off by Price had completely subsided, Boswell and Johnson talked about the population of London. Johnson said it was not growing. Boswell mentioned Price's view that considering the high mortality rate, those who survived were "as stout and strong people as any." Johnson agreed with this thesis of natural selection.[6] In 1794 Lord Stanhope, a friend of parliamentary reform and an associate of Price in the Revolution Society, wrote to Wilberforce concerning the military power of France, and he cited Price's figures to show that France's thirty million inhabitants outnumbered those of England and Wales six to one.

It was ironical that Price, so pacific and equable, had a genius for starting controversies. The one that followed his population writings was not the last he began. In the summer of 1779 William Morgan published a *Treatise on the Doctrine of Annuities* . . . to which was appended Price's *An Essay on the Present State of Population in England and Wales*. Price assisted his nephew in the preparation of the *Treatise*, and since the actuarial science was so closely related to the population problem, he took the opportunity of including his *Essay* in Morgan's book. His statements regarding the decline of the population evoked criticisms. William Eden, who was to become identified with the commercial policies of the government under Pitt the Younger, wrote one of the replies. In a

[5] (3 vols., London, 1774), I, 36.
[6] Shorter (ed.), *Life of Johnson*, VIII, 3.

pamphlet called *Fifth Letter to Lord Carlisle*, Eden made several objections to Price's remarks. Price thereupon published his essay separately, with an appendix specifically directed in rebuttal to Eden. The *Essay* appeared in May, 1780, and a month later a second edition was printed.[7]

The *Essay* is interesting today not so much for its figures on population as for its illustration of statistical methodology in this precensus era. Price started with the hearth-tax returns since the Revolution of 1688, comparing them with the window and house-tax returns of his own day. He stubbornly refused to admit what some of his contemporaries well knew. These records were notoriously defective, for many householders succeeded in avoiding taxes and the window-tax surveyors omitted certain classifications. Price also employed miscellaneous information concerning mortality, colonial migration, agricultural enclosures, and the growth of London. Then he added his own speculations about the debilitating effects of luxury and urbanization. Out of this mixture of erroneous statistics and gloomy social philosophy came false conclusions. In round numbers he estimated one million dwellings and five persons in each, or a total population for England and Wales of five million.[8] These were smaller than the comparable figures for 1690.

After demonstrating the decline of population, Price analyzed the reasons for it. The most important were the increase of the armed forces, emigration, enclosures, high prices of provisions, the growth of luxury, and the increases of debts and taxes. All of these directly or indirectly discouraged marriage, made it difficult to rear families, and in various other ways reduced the birth rate. Price could not prove that the birth rate was declining, and he ignored the important fact that the death rate was diminishing. If the birth rate remained unchanged, or even if it fell, the remarkable decline of the

[7] The full title is *An Essay on the Population of England, from the Revolution to the present Time. With an appendix, containing Remarks on the Account of the Population, Trade, and Resources of the Kingdom, in Mr. Eden's letters to Lord Carlisle.*

[8] *Essay*, 6, 12, 13, 78.

mortality rate would have resulted in a population increase. In fact, the birth rate increased from 31.1 in 1700 to 35.44 per thousand in 1790.[9] Except for a few years in the second quarter of the century, the death rate was significantly lower than the birth rate. Allowing that the birth rate increased but slowly, "It is not so much the fact that people were born into the world which accounts for the population changes of the eighteenth century as that more of those who were born survived the perils of infancy and reached adult life."[10]

Eden and Price differed about population figures without becoming angry. They corresponded occasionally on matters relating to their mutual interests in trade, public finance, and population. They were searching for the truth rather than attempting to convert one another. The difficulties they met looking for valid statistics of trade, as well as the spirit in which they disagreed, were illustrated by a letter from Price to Eden written January 4, 1780.

> M[r] [John] Lee having convey'd to me your letter to him, I cannot make myself easy without sending you my thanks for the candour with which you have received my remarks; a candour which I wish to imitate. What I said of the quantity of tea paying duty consumed in the kingdom was too hasty. My only *datum* for determining this was the produce of the customs and excise on tea; but had I attended to this with more care, I might have concluded that the quantity of tea paying duty must have been more nearly as you give it. Still, however, I must think that any estimate of the tea smuggled which makes it greater than or near as much as the tea that pays duty, exceeds too much all the bounds of credibility. . . . Under a grateful sense of your civility . . . etc.[11]

Several others differed publicly with Price. The Reverend John Howlett, the most dispassionate of all, admitted that neither side in the controversy could prove its case, for he

---

[9] Dietz, *Economic History*, 282.   [10] *Ibid*
[11] British Museum, Additional Manuscripts, 34,417, F. 12.

entitled his second pamphlet: *Uncertainty of the present Population of the Kingdom, deduced from a candid review of the accounts lately given of it by Dr. Price on the one hand, and Mr. Eden, Mr. Wales, and Mr. Howlett on the other* (1781). Howlett estimated the population lay between eight and nine million, which was as far on one side of the mark as Price was on the other.

The Abbé Morellet did not enter the dispute, but in a letter to Shelburne he criticized intelligently Price's methodology. He said that one must be careful to use valid data in problems of political arithmetic. He did not see how Price's calculations could be accurate if they were based only on the number of houses. Nevertheless, concluded the Abbé, Price deserved commendation, for considering all of his writings upon various questions, his country and his century owed him much.[12]

Howlett and the Abbé just about summed up the population discussion. Even if a man happened to hit upon the correct figure, he had no way of proving he was right. Sufficient data simply did not exist. The controversy, however, hastened the day when adequate statistics would be available, and so if Price's results were erroneous, his work was nonetheless important.

In his *Essay,* Price discussed another of his chronic worries, the national debt. This problem was no different than before, only more urgent because of the swelling of the debt during the war. Increased taxes were inevitable, and with them must come the ruinous social consequences that Price had been dreading for a decade. It seemed necessary to call attention to the debt once again.

In 1780 Price published his latest reflections on the subject on national finance in an anonymous pamphlet attacking the North ministry for its misguided and dangerous financial policies. The book was ostensibly directed to the people of

[12] Fitzmaurice (ed), *Lettres de Morellet,* 170-72, letter of August 25, 1779. Morellet was writing about Price's essay appended to Morgan's *Treatise on Annuities.*

England, but more particularly, as its title makes clear, to the wealthier classes. It was called *Facts: Addressed to the Landholders, Stockholders, Merchants, Farmers, Manufacturers, Tradesmen, Proprietors of every Description, and generally to all The Subjects of Great Britain and Ireland.* Selling for only two shillings and containing some pungent charges against the ministry, it quickly ran through eight editions.

The authorship of the pamphlet was a well advertised secret. Two notorious radicals, John Horne Tooke and Dr. Richard Price had written it. The collaboration of Tooke and Price was a strange one, allowing even for their complete agreement upon political matters. Tooke is remembered as a gadfly on the English body politic. A nervy man with a genius for self-advertisement, and possessing a special ability for making himself obnoxious to men in public office, Tooke, before he died in 1812, acquired an intimate knowledge of the insides of jails. His father, a well-to-do poulterer, sent him to Westminster, Eton (where he lost an eye in a fracas with a knife-wielding scholar), and Cambridge. In 1760, two years after receiving his A.B. degree, Tooke was ordained an Anglican clergyman. During the next decade he actively supported John Wilkes, though they quarreled later. In 1778 he went to prison for having promoted a subscription for the relatives of Americans "barbarously murdered at Lexington by the King's soldiers in 1775."[13]

Tooke doubtless developed some unkind feelings toward the North government during his imprisonment, yet it would be mistaking his character to assume that he wrote the *Facts* out of a desire for personal revenge. He was as sincere a supporter of what he considered the cause of civil liberty as the man with whom he collaborated. Moreover, he supported the reform movement during the French Revolution when, after 1792, anyone who advocated parliamentary reform endangered his life. Tooke was one of the famous Twelve who stood trial for high treason in 1794 because they criticized the unrepresentative character of Parliament.

---

[13] Joseph Greig (ed.), *The Farington Diary* (4th ed., 8 vols., London, 1923), I, 79 n. The article on Tooke in *D.N.B.* contains slightly different phrasing.

While Price enjoyed attacking the North ministry, this does not explain how he became an associate of Tooke. Their common exertions in favor of America doubtless made them known to one another, but there seems to be no record of their meeting or agreeing to write a book. Neither is there any explanation of Shelburne's opposition to the publication of the pamphlet, although he supplied Price and Tooke with some of their information.[14] Price preferred to accede to Shelburne's wishes, but the bold Tooke persisted in carrying out the project. Shelburne's anger against Tooke never abated.[15] When he was prime minister two years later, he successfully opposed Tooke's call to the bar of the Inner Temple. He stood on a technicality, but he detested Tooke.

Price and Tooke intended to reveal how the corrupt ministry of Lord North wasted and misspent public moneys during the war. Nothing in the pamphlet was out of harmony with the spirit or content of Dunning's resolution. Both were products of the same rising tide of opposition to government methods and policies. Colonel Barré in the House of Commons had already attacked the contract for supplying rum to the armed forces; in December, 1779, the Duke of Richmond and Earl Shelburne in the House of Lords called for the cessation of waste, reduction of the civil list, an examination of public accounts, and the making of public contracts; and Burke, on February 11, 1780, introduced his plan of economical reform for curing England of the disease of rotten government by reducing "that corrupt influence which is itself the perennial spring of all prodigality and of all disorder,—which loads us more than millions of debt,—which takes away the vigor from our arms, wisdom from our councils, and every shadow of authority and credit from the most venerable parts of our Constitution."[16] The *Facts* was in tune with the spirit of criticism abroad in the land.

Price wrote the second and eighth chapters, which were concerned primarily with financial matters. Tooke introduced

14 Minnie Clare Yarborough, *John Horne Tooke* (New York, 1926), 98.
15 Fitzmaurice, *Shelburne*, III, 96.
16 *Works* (12 vols., Boston, 1884), II, 267.

the subject by referring to the demands of Richmond and
Shelburne, ending by asking anyone who doubted the need
for reform candidly to examine the facts. Price described
how the principal of the national debt had increased since
1775 by £47,437,500 and the annual charge by £1,842,000. In
order to manage the new debt, there must be levied additional
taxes to return annually £700,000.[17] Price concluded his first
contribution by showing how heavy taxes destroyed prosperity
and threatened to produce rebellion.

Tooke continued the attack. He compared the financial
conditions of the French and English governments, asserting
that as a result of some recent reforms, the French government was better off financially than the English. He dismissed
the royal promise of economy as an empty gesture. He attacked Lord North for circumventing parliamentary control
of army expenditures. But the juicy bit for which Tooke saved
his scorn was the rum contract for the army. He told the livid
details of the swindle worked by the contractor, Charles At-
kinson, whose verbal agreement with North was unknown to
the Treasury for two years. Besides this scandal, other mal-
practices when taken together were of considerable significance. For all of them the North administration was culpable.

In the eighth chapter, Price flailed the borrowing policy
of North, who had permitted the nation to fall prey to loan
contractors. The loan of 1779 was most objectionable. Price
accused North of failing to secure terms as favorable as he
could have gained, though North pleaded in Parliament that
they were the best he could get and that in time of war con-
tracting was preferable to open subscription. Price said the
public had been misled, for the loan figured out to 6½ per
cent interest instead of the supposed 5 per cent.[18] And there
was scant prospect that the loan of 1780 would be any better.[19]

[17] *Facts*, 17, 18.

[18] *Ibid.*, 106. Also Hargreaves, *The National Debt*, 67.

[19] The £12,000,000 loan of 1780 was contracted under slightly different
terms, but hardly more favorable for the government. North confessed that
he had again been at the mercy of loan contractors. Hargreaves, *The National
Debt*, 67-68, *Parl. Paper*, 1898, [C.-9010], 30.

The inference was clear that a change of ministers was needed.

This hot-blooded pamphlet drove home two lessons: the exorbitant influence of the crown was dangerous; reform of Parliament and the high offices of state was imperative.

The opposition which tumbled North's ministry in 1782 had benefited by the circumstances of the previous two years. The decline of England's prestige had favored its growth. The pamphlet of Price and Tooke, which sold eight editions, hurt North. In fact, Franklin congratulated Price for assisting in the overthrow of North, saying that the power of the press could be enormous when used opportunely.[20] The cry for reform was not an expedient used only for the purpose of ousting North. The actions of the short Rockingham ministry proved its sincerity. In 1782 it enacted Burke's economical reform, thereby purging the administration of many corruptions that have never reappeared. The national revival promoted by the zealous statesmanship of the younger Pitt during the early peacetime years of his long ministry showed the tenacity of the reform spirit. Price had a part in the reconstruction work undertaken by Pitt.

The brief administration of the Marquis of Rockingham ended with the death of the prime minister in July, 1782. While some important reforms had been undertaken, there had not been time, had there been the inclination, to grapple with the problem of the national debt. That problem loomed large by the time Shelburne became prime minister, and for the attention which was now being paid to the debt question, Price was in large part responsible. His writings on the national debt were more widely read than any similar writings of the last half of the eighteenth century.[21] Not only did Price do much to awaken public interest to the dangers of a large debt, but he had direct influence upon two prime ministers who listened earnestly to his pleadings. Shelburne had been for more than a decade in the tutelage of Price, and now, in 1782, he was in a position to promote measures for

---

[20] Bigelow, *Franklin*, VII, 470-71.
[21] Hargreaves, *The National Debt*, 91.

handling the debt problem. The King's Speech of December 5, 1782, gave assurance that the ministry was contemplating a program for managing the debt.[22]

As it turned out, the Shelburne ministry had to resign in February, 1783. Led by Fox and North, the House of Commons disapproved of the conduct of the peace negotiations which had monopolized the government's attention. Though the Shelburne ministry failed to bring to completion its financial schemes, it nevertheless made a start on the debt problem.

The Shelburne Papers show that during the decade preceding his ministry, Shelburne had been studying public finance. Volume 117, entitled "Revenue Notes & Calculations by Dr. Price," is a miscellany. One paper, dated November, 1761, contains an account of government finance as Price envisaged it for the following year, and stressed the importance of the Sinking Fund. On February 11, 1762, Price expressed fears of national bankruptcy for the next year. These papers preceded the publication of Price's *Observations on Reversionary Payments* by ten years. How they came to be in the Shelburne Papers is a puzzle, for Price did not meet Shelburne for another six years.

In this volume there is also a paper, undated but probably written about 1775, containing sketches of plans for managing the debt. One plan called for a new Sinking Fund to be administered by a Board of Commissioners. Another paper criticized the plan offered by Price in his *Appeal to the Public, on the Subject of the National Debt*. The writer did not question the mathematics of Price's plan but only doubted whether ministers would apply it faithfully, citing Price's history of the Sinking Fund of 1716. Thus, during these years before he came to power, Shelburne was seriously studying the debt question.

As prime minister, Shelburne considered various plans for handling the debt. He received much gratuitous, but not al-

[22] *Parl. Hist.*, XXIII, 208 There are in the Shelburne Papers, vol. 168, four drafts of this speech. The paragraph relating to the national debt underwent some change in wording among these drafts, but none in its sense.

ways disinterested, advice. One James Macobee on March 30, 1782, submitted to Shelburne an elaborate plan for raising money by levying fees upon wagons and barges.[23] Wyndham Madden and a M. Herrenschwand also sent plans to Shelburne. The most insistent self-appointed adviser was E. Lonsbergs, a lawyer of Maestricht, who early in 1783 wrote several letters to Shelburne containing ideas for redeeming the national debt. He must have been a magnanimous gentleman, for he was willing to come to London to advise Shelburne—provided his expenses were paid.[24]

The person in whom Shelburne placed most confidence was, of course, Dr. Price. Within a month after becoming prime minister, with William Pitt the Younger as chancellor of the exchequer, Shelburne sought Price's aid, evidently after discussion with Pitt.[25] Price returned the plan submitted to him for criticism, with the comment that Mr. Pitt "does me great honor by supposing me capable of being of any use to him." He did not like the scheme suggested, for it operated too slowly and did not take sufficient advantage of the working of compound interest. He went on to emphasize the provisions he thought should be in a sound Sinking Fund plan.

Within the next few months, Price submitted a plan of his own, probably upon the request of Shelburne and Pitt. The authority for this statement does not exist in the Shelburne or Chatham Papers, but other evidence is conclusive. At the time of its fall, the Shelburne administration "had under consideration a plan . . . [for managing the debt] which is laid before the Public in these papers." This statement occurs in the introduction to Price's *The State of the Public Debts and Finances at signing the Preliminary Articles of Peace in January, 1783. With a Plan for raising money by public loans, and for redeeming the public debts.* The pamphlet, published in 1783, went into a second edition. After the fall of the Fox-North ministry in December, 1783, Price published a

[23] Shelburne Papers, vol. 135.   [24] *Ibid.*
[25] Chatham Papers, Public Record Office, G. D. 8/169, Price to Shelburne, August 6, 1782.

postscript in the hopes of impressing the new prime minister, Pitt the Younger, with the gravity of the debt problem.

Price had two purposes: to give an accurate statement of the debt situation as of January, 1783; and now that the war was being concluded and perhaps an era of peace setting in, to suggest an easily workable plan for managing the debt and handling new loans. He said the debt was £252,584,986, of which not quite half had been contracted since midsummer of 1775.[26] Financial statistics for the eighteenth century were notoriously inconsistent, but Price's figures were widely accepted, and they agree fairly closely with later computations.[27] J. Holland Rose called Price "one of the closest students of finance," and in his discussion of the debt question for this period he used Price's figures.[28]

Price nowhere stated how he obtained his totals or what methods he used. Certainly Shelburne made many records available to him. The difficulties involved in the task of preparing a statement of the debt indicate the amount of labor Price spent in compiling his statistics, and should increase respect for his work. The National Debt Office, when preparing its *Report* of 1898, had available not only its trained clerical staff, but it also had much readier access to all the documents. In his "Memorandum" to the *Report*, Mr. G. Hervey, comptroller general, said:

> The information has in the main been compiled from original records of Income and Expenditure at the Public Record Offices of England and Ireland; and it is hoped that the details now given may be found helpful in explaining other published figures relating to the Debt, which, owing to the different methods of compilation adopted, occasionally show apparent divergencies.

[26] *State of the Public Debts*, 8. Also *ibid.*, 5-6.

[27] Compare with the figures given in Hargreaves, *The National Debt*, 5, 72, and the *Report* of the National Debt Office presented to Parliament in 1898, *Parl. Paper* [C.-9010], 31, 33. The variations are surprisingly slight, considering the intricacies involved in compiling the scattered and miscellaneous records of the period prior to 1786.

[28] *William Pitt and National Revival* (London, 1911), 179-80.

No separate abstract of the Loans comprised in this Statement of the Funded Debt is to be found in any of the early records; and in order to arrive at the total amount of the Funded Debt at the 29th September, 1786, the figures have been extracted from year to year from a mass of entries, particulars of the several Loans being verified by reference to the Acts of Parliament authorizing them.

. . . The result as printed gives but an imperfect idea of the time and labour involved in the investigation; and [Mr. A. T. King, chief clerk] deserves the greatest credit for having thrown so clear a light on a difficult and obscure period of the National Debt.

A difference of a few million pounds one way or the other matters little to Price's major contention, that the debt had become so huge as to endanger the security of the nation. The growth of the debt meant an increase in the annual charge for the debt service, and in consequence an enlargement of the tax burden upon the people. Nevertheless, the situation was not beyond recovery. Estimating annual expenditures at £13,856,931, Price calculated that the revenue system would return £12,399,575 annually, leaving a deficiency of £1,459,356 each year. Allowing for an increase of revenue with the return of peace and commercial expansion, and setting aside one million a year for a Sinking Fund, Price thought that new taxes returning £1,700,686 annually would be adequate.[29]

But there was no time to be lost in placing England's financial house in order. "If, before another war begins, the revenue is not re-instated, the public debts put into a *fixed* course of payment, and some progress made in reducing them, it is impossible but the catastrophe must come towards which we have been for some time advancing."[30] The Shelburne ministry had under advisement Price's scheme for managing the debt, but having been forced out of office by the machinations of "a coalition of parties which sickens every honest man," no action had been taken. "I drew up the following sketch,

---

[29] *State of the Public Debts*, 11, 12.   [30] *Ibid.*, 18.

and submitted it to the consideration of the king's ministry," and though the ministry is no longer in office, there can be "no impropriety in laying it before the public."[31]

Naturally Price proposed a Sinking Fund, to which a million annually would be dedicated. This surplus was to come from economies and new taxes. To render the fund more effective, the interest on the national debt ought to be increased from 3 per cent to 4 per cent, thereby enabling the magic of compound interest to work an even greater miracle. A Sinking Fund of a million a year could, in the same period, retire £33,000,000 more of a 4 per cent than of a 3 per cent debt. This, admitted Price, sounded paradoxical to the uninitiated who had no conception of the powers of compound interest. The conversion to a higher interest rate and the funding of the floating debt would fix the total at £183,000,000, which the Sinking Fund would retire in fifty years. Shelburne had all this in mind when on May 5, 1783, he moved that all future loans be handled in a manner conducive to the best management of the debt.[32]

This obsession with the working of compound interest rates was precisely what led Price astray. As a mathematical proposition, compound interest does make a small initial quantity increase with amazing rapidity. But government finance is quite a different thing. Only a clear surplus of revenue over expenditure can reduce a public debt. That surplus has to come from taxes paid either directly or indirectly by the people. If the rate of interest on the public debt is high, as Price wanted it to be, the ultimate cost to the taxpayer will be much greater than if it is low; if the fund seems to grow faster when stocks bear a high rate of interest, that is because the taxpayer has paid more than if the rate is low. The gain to the nation is illusory, for the accumulating dividends from retired stock, paid to Sinking Fund Commissioners instead of to the public creditors, are not derived from investment in a productive enterprise but from taxation. So long as a clear

[31] *Ibid.*, 18, 19.   [32] *Ibid.*, 32.

surplus of revenue exists, a Sinking Fund is neither good nor evil so far as it retires debt or relieves the burden of taxes. The greatest advantage of an inviolable Sinking Fund in time of peace and when a surplus exists is psychological, since it emphasizes the debt continually, and mechanical, since it provides for systematic retirement of the debt. Price should have stressed the psychological aspect more than he did, but he was entranced by the mathematical operation of compound interest. And so in one book after another he perpetuated his misconception and imposed it upon others, including William Pitt the Younger.

Pitt became prime minister in December, 1783, succeeding the short-lived Fox-North coalition. By winning the election of 1784 Pitt ensured himself a long tenure. After fifteen years of exhortation, Price was at last to be rewarded. In September, 1785, Pitt wrote to his good friend William Wilberforce, "I am half mad with a project which will give our supplies the effect almost of magic in the reduction of debt."[33] The project was a Sinking Fund which had "fired Pitt with hope."[34]

[33] Rose, *Pitt and National Revival*, 188.   [34] *Ibid.*, 180.

Chapter XI

THE SINKING FUND

ONE of the major tasks confronting Pitt when he became prime minister was introducing order into the management of public finance. He grappled with the problem at once. Whatever he did about improving the methods of borrowing money, funding the unfunded debt, raising the interest rate on government stocks, or consolidating the revenue (which he accomplished after establishing the Sinking Fund) was always with the ultimate view of facilitating the redemption of the public debt. In the famous speech of June 30, 1784, he revealed his plan of finance. If his remarks were not derived from Price's teachings, they certainly bore a remarkable similarity to ideas Price had been expounding since Pitt's schooldays. Pitt said,

> It was always my idea that a fund at a high rate of interest is better to the country than those at low rates; that a four per cent. is preferable to a three per cent., and a five per cent. better than four. The reason is that in all operations of finance we should always have in view a plan of redemption. Gradually to redeem and to extinguish our debt ought ever to be the wise pursuit of Government. Every scheme and operation of finance should be directed to that end, and managed with that view.[1]

During the next year and a half Pitt showed his determination to proceed with plans for redeeming the debt. As early as June 23, 1784, George Dempster, who was close to Pitt, in the

---

[1] Quoted in Earl Stanhope, *Life of the Right Honourable William Pitt* (4 vols., London, 1861-1862), I, 219.

House of Commons praised the Sinking Fund idea, following "that able calculator Dr. Price."[2] In January, 1785, Pitt spoke of the successes of his new financial program and promised that in the next year a Sinking Fund would be established.[3] He carried through additional taxes preparatory to acquiring a surplus for a new fund. On April 11 he gave out more financial information in order that members could inform themselves "on a subject, which was nearest to his heart."[4] This was the project with which, Pitt was soon to write Wilberforce, he was "half mad."

Price's reputation as an authority upon public finance was already well known to Pitt. In 1784, when arranging for the new loan, Pitt had received Price's suggestions.[5] During the next year Price continued to study financial policy. On April 28, 1785, he wrote to John Wilkes apologizing for the delay in sending him certain papers.[6] They had been "for some time in Mr. Pitt's hands; but Dr. Price does not know how far the plan they contain will or will not be adopted." A little later, Price wrote to Eden concerning some financial accounts.[7] Eden was in Pitt's confidence, and Price mentioned to him the dangers of a huge public debt.

Soon Pitt was ready to consider specific suggestions. On January 8, 1786, he sent the outline of a plan to Price for his study and comment.[8] Said Pitt, "Before I form any decisive opinion, I wish to learn your sentiments upon it, and I shall think myself obliged to you for any improvement you can suggest if you can think the principle a right one, or any other

---

[2] *Parl. Hist.*, XXIV, 1014   [3] Stanhope, *Pitt*, I, 255.

[4] *Parl. Hist*, XXV, 420.

[5] Chatham Papers, Public Record Office, G.D. 8/169, letter from Price to Pitt. June 7, 1784.

[6] British Museum, Add. MSS., 30,872, F. 266.

[7] *Ibid.*, 34,420, F. 29, letter of June 11, 1785.

[8] Price, *Observations on Reversionary Payments* (7th ed.), I, 319-20. Morgan, the editor of this edition, tells the story of the Sinking Fund. I do not understand Professor Rose's statement that no comparison of Pitt's and Price's plans is possible because Morgan omitted a description of Pitt's scheme. Rose, *Pitt and National Revival*, 191. Rose, I believe, underestimates the importance of Price's part in creating the Sinking Fund.

proposal which from your knowledge of the subject you may think preferable."[9] Price promised to give his opinion as soon as possible, and he "rejoyced to find that you intend this season to establish a plan of redemption."[10] Three days later he sent Pitt some conversion and Sinking Fund tables that he considered more effective than the ones Pitt had sent to him.[11] He asked him for a few more days in which to study, as he wanted to be certain of his verdict.

In the meantime, Pitt was drafting the royal speech. He sent a rough copy to the king who, on January 14, approved the phraseology of the part referring to the plan for reduction of the debt.[12] Price spent the interval in hard work, and on January 19 he had an interview with Pitt. Price argued so convincingly for the superiority of his own plans to Pitt's, that the prime minister asked him to draw up in detail the three alternative plans he had in mind.

Price was prepared for such a request. He promptly sent Pitt a paper entitled "Three Plans for shewing the progress and effect during 40 years of a Fund consisting of a million *per ann* aided as is therein expressed, and apply'd to the redemption of the public debts."[13] The plans and the explanatory notes are in Price's handwriting. Plan I provided for a surplus of a million a year, to be augmented from time to time by savings from the falling in of various annuities and their expenses of management, and also for the conversion of £60,000,000 of the 3 per cents into 4 per cents. The difference in annual interest payments was to be paid by the returns of new taxes, to the amount of £600,000 a year. This fund

[9] Quoted in Rose, *Pitt and National Revival*, 190.

[10] Chatham Papers, G.D. 8/169, letter of January 9, 1786.

[11] *Ibid.* The tables are *ibid.*, G.D. 8/275.

[12] Correspondence of King George III, vol. II, 507, transcripts by Sir John Fortescue in the William L. Clements Library.

[13] Chatham Papers, G.D. 8/275. These plans, also given by Morgan in the *Observations on Reversionary Payments* (7th ed.), I, 322-39, are to be distinguished from the tables Price had sent previously to Pitt. The paper containing these plans is dated January, 1786, but the precise date lies between January 19 and February 1, for on the latter date Price mentions these plans as already having been sent to Pitt. Chatham Papers, G.D. 8/169.

at the end of forty years, would have redeemed £188,585,873 of debt. Plan II omitted the conversion scheme, but the million surplus and the additions to it from the falling in of annuities were to be aided by £600,000 to be raised within the first five years by new taxes or by economies. This fund would redeem £171,522,335 of debt at the end of forty years. Plan III was the simplest and least heroic, and was the one most nearly like the Sinking Fund adopted. It required only the million annual surplus aided by the savings from the retirement of annuities, without contemplating either conversions or new taxes. Price calculated that in forty years it would extinguish £126,070,401 of debt.

Price preferred the first plan. In his explanatory notes he argued that conversions would give confidence to the public in the beginning, when there might be apprehensions about the redemption plan. Also, this plan would operate more vigorously from the outset, and if interrupted, would have accomplished much more in the same period than either of the other plans. For example, if terminated in the seventh year, it would have redeemed £25,000,000 of debt, while Plan II would have retired less than half that sum in the same length of time. Price argued further that Plan I would bring the 5 per cents into a course of redemption at the end of six years, whereas Plan II would not do this for thirteen years and Plan III not for sixteen.

Pitt now undertook a serious study of Price's proposals. The King's Speech of January 24 made it clear that a redemption plan was to be laid before Parliament.[14] Price seemed to have no doubts of the sincerity of Pitt's intentions, though he was unsettled concerning Pitt's decision among the three plans. On February 1 he sent another table to the prime minister. In the accompanying letter, while saying he thought the business in good hands, he urged that a measure so efficacious as the one in his third table (which corresponded to Plan I) be "considered and left open to adoption."[15]

[14] *Parl Hist.*, XXV, 986.   [15] Chatham Papers, G.D. 8/169.

The draft bill similar to Plan III was soon drawn up; Price received a copy; after studying it he wrote to Pitt on February 12, saying he would call upon the prime minister at 11 a.m. the next Wednesday.[16] In his letter he urged the necessity of adopting strong measures, meaning his first plan. He objected seriously only to one part of the bill as drawn. Section 10 provided for the cessation of additions to the fund after it had grown to the amount of £4,000,000 of free revenue, that is, after twenty-seven years. Price was disappointed because the fund would be impeded in its operations just at the time that the workings of compound interest were becoming most effective. He thought, however, that the incorporation of three other items would strengthen the plan: specification of the order in which the different classes of debt were to be redeemed; additional safeguards for keeping the fund inviolate; and a sketch of the progress of the fund so that people might see in advance how it would accumulate. But even without these, the bill established the principle of the Sinking Fund, which would always reflect credit upon Pitt's administration.

Price still thought he could persuade Pitt to adopt the most instead of the least efficacious of his three plans. In a paper entitled "Queries," he re-emphasized the desirability of taking the fullest advantage of the workings of compound interest and repeated that early vigor in the operation of a Sinking Fund was desirable.[17] In yet another paper, Price suggested alterations in the discretionary powers of the commissioners who were to control the fund.[18] Pitt was not impressed by Price's suggestions. He had no stomach for another stiff increase in taxes, which Price's first two plans called for. The draft bill was not changed, but before it was introduced, a select committee to examine the revenue was appointed. Its report set the annual revenue at £15,397,471 and estimated

---

[16] *Ibid.*

[17] *Ibid.*, G.D. 8/275. This paper, undated, falls within the period prior to the introduction of the bill in Commons, March 29.

[18] *Ibid.*

expenditures at £14,478,181.[19] This difference was just a little short of the £1,000,000 clear surplus that was needed for the Sinking Fund.

March 29 was the big day. In a masterly exposition upon the state of English finance, Pitt recommended that the surplus of £1,000,000 a year be paid over in quarterly installments to a Board of Commissioners.[20] The fund was to be augmented periodically by the interest of the stocks redeemed until it reached a total of £4,000,000. Thereafter the cumulative operation ceased, the interest on stock henceforth purchased by the commissioners would not be applied to the fund, and the debt would simply be canceled as stock was bought up. Since the select committee had revealed that the expected annual surplus was just short of £1,000,000, Pitt proposed excise taxes to raise the additional £100,000 required.[21] Finally, Pitt insisted upon the inviolability of the fund. In fact, there was no way of keeping the fund inviolate, as Fox pointed out, because any Parliament could undo the acts of a previous one.

During the month of April the plan not only was debated in Commons, but underwent further discussion among Pitt's advisers. On April 17, Price met with a delegation, including Sir John Sinclair, Sir Edward Ferguson, Henry Beaufoy, and George Dempster, and they discussed the official scheme as well as one suggested by a Mr. Gale.[22] No essential changes were made in the plan as it passed through its parliamentary course. Perhaps Pitt was using Price as an interpreter to some of his advisers who had doubts or questions; Dempster, however, needed no convincing.

Earl Stanhope was the outstanding opponent of Pitt's bill in the House of Lords, as Fox had been in Commons. Stanhope did not oppose the principle of the bill; rather he believed that it did not go far enough.[23] He favored a conversion

[19] Hargreaves, *The National Debt*, 89.   [20] *Parl. Hist.*, XXV, 1294-1312.

[21] Hargreaves, *The National Debt*, 100.

[22] Rose, *Pitt and National Revival*, 191. This was probably Samuel Gale, for whom see Dorfman, *The Economic Mind*, I, 229-38.

[23] *Parl. Hist.*, XXVI, 17-26.

scheme to supplement the Sinking Fund, much as contemplated in Price's first plan. In one of his speeches, he read a letter dated May 15, 1786, in which Price had written, "The plan which Mr. Pitt has adopted is that which I have been writing about, and recommending for several years," but Price went on to say that Pitt's bill did not satisfy him entirely, because of the provision for checking the growth of the fund after the sum of £4,000,000 had been attained. That is, Price was gratified to see Pitt adopt the basic principle, but was disappointed that the more efficacious plan had not been accepted. The bill passed by Parliament, and accepted by the king on May 26, was essentially the plan introduced on March 29, which in its broader aspects, though not in all its details, was Price's Plan III.

There has been some difference of opinion concerning Price's role in the establishment of the Sinking Fund. William Morgan was incensed because Pitt did not openly acknowledge the obligations Morgan thought he owed to Price; J. Holland Rose, the biographer of Pitt, minimizes the significance of Price's assistance.[24] Rose's exoneration of Pitt from charges of ingratitude rests mainly upon the contention that Pitt owed little to Price for his thinking about public finance. An apologist for Pitt has difficulty in proving such a case, though he might show that Pitt was not so deluded as Price over compound interest. It might be franker to reason, with only circumstantial evidence for support, that Pitt saw no need for publicly expressing obligation to Price since it was no secret that Price had been consulted frequently. If this is true, it is still not a strong justification for Pitt's omission of Price's name in the parliamentary debates.

The questions remain: was Price responsible for convincing Pitt of the need of a Sinking Fund, and was the bill as passed consonant with the plan Price originally proposed? The evidence already presented would seem to order affirmative answers, and Professor Rose's defense of Pitt does not, therefore,

24 Rose, *Pitt and National Revival*, 191-92.

convince. It is difficult to trace the evolution of a man's thought and to assess accurately the significance of each of the various influences that mold his mind. Yet some suggestions can be made. Adam Smith, to whose influence Pitt made acknowledgments, was not in favor of a Sinking Fund. Price had long been the most persistent advocate of precisely those ideas of public finance that Pitt embraced, particularly the conversion of government stocks into issues bearing higher rates of interest, and the Sinking Fund. During the formative period of Pitt's life, Price championed these measures; when Pitt was Shelburne's chancellor of the exchequer, he heard Price's suggestions for a conversion program and the establishment of a Sinking Fund; and when Pitt became prime minister he carried these plans into effect, at least in their broad aspects, after dropping his own plan for a Sinking Fund when Price criticized it. If Pitt did not confess owing anything to Price during the parliamentary discussions, the expressions in his private correspondence with Price were clear. Or else Pitt was a hypocrite. On the whole it seems fair to say that in his general view of financial policy, "Pitt was obviously under the influence of Price's doctrines."[25]

The evidence also reveals a close resemblance between Price's third plan and the Sinking Fund that was established. Price's writings had revived the popularity of the old Sinking Fund idea, to which he had added his own emphasis upon compound interest, and he was universally admitted to be the outstanding supporter of it. There was little doubt among his contemporaries on this point. Soon after the bill passed, Shelburne wrote that as long as England had a Sinking Fund, Price's name would be connected with it.[26] Perfectly and ironically true. When the fund was attacked during and after the Napoleonic Wars, Price as much as Pitt was a culprit. The reason was that "The system of finance recommended by Dr. Price, is the same as that carried into execution under the administration of Mr. Pitt, and continued since."[27]

[25] Hargreaves, *The National Debt*, 104.   [26] M.H S.P. (1903), 351.
[27] Robert Hamilton, *An Inquiry concerning the Rise and Progress, the Re-*

In the course of its operation the Sinking Fund did not ful-
fill the high expectations of its founders.[28] For a while it worked
according to plan, and by February 1, 1793, had paid off
£10,242,100 of the 3 per cents.[29]

Later critics pointed out, however, that the apparent success of the fund in these years of peace was due simply to the
existence of the clear surplus which, without the mechanism
of the Sinking Fund, would have extinguished debt anyway.
A different allegation about the fund is impossible either to
refute or prove, though it may be denied. After the war began
the existence of the fund helped maintain faith in public
credit and "made possible the negotiation on favourable terms
of fresh loans."[30]

One heavy attack upon the operation of the Sinking Fund
used the argument that the commissioners, in order to prevent
the interruption of the workings of the fund after war came
and the surplus of revenues over expenditures melted away,
borrowed at high rates of interest to maintain a fund that
was retiring debt bearing a lower rate of interest. The interest on new loans accumulated in the same way as did the
interest on debt bought up by the commissioners. While the
defect of this expedient is obvious, and while Price had insisted upon the desirability of such a procedure as a means
of preserving the continuity of the cumulative action, he
had never contemplated this except as a temporary expedient.
Neither he nor anyone else foresaw a war lasting twenty-two
years. If the ministry had possessed the courage to increase
taxes sufficiently to meet the charges on new loans for the
Sinking Fund, the plan would have worked. Again, however,
success would have been due to the existence of a real surplus
raised by taxes rather than to the magic of the Sinking Fund.

---

*demption and Present State, and the Management of the National Debt of
Great Britain* (Edinburgh, 1813), 141. This was the most devastating attack
upon the Fund and upon Price's ideas.

[28] Shelburne Papers, vol. 135, contains an account of the Fund, in Price's
hand, dated July 3, 1789. Evidently Price was watching its progress. The
history of the Fund is given in *Parl. Paper*, 1891 [C.-6539], 7-33.

[29] Hargreaves, *The National Debt*, 105.   [30] *Ibid.*, 106.

Apart from his entrancement with compound interest, Price's greatest miscalculation was his confidence that a long era of peace was at hand, and that even if a war occurred, it would not last for more than two decades. It is unfair to blame him for this. When the Sinking Fund began in 1786, there seemed every reason to believe that a durable peace had arrived. England was recovering from the decline she had suffered as a result of the American Revolution. Relations with France were good; in fact, a commercial treaty, providing for a mutual lowering of restrictive duties, was concluded just two months after the Sinking Fund began operations. There was justification for thinking that the future would be better than the past. If trade continued to increase and peace endured, a continual surplus of revenue over expenditures would exist. Under these conditions, the Sinking Fund would have done its work, though not because of Price's compound interest. But who, in 1786, had ever heard of Bonaparte?

CHAPTER XII

AFFAIRS PUBLIC AND PRIVATE

THE decade of the 1780's opened and closed amidst excitement in England concerning public affairs. The relatively quiet middle years saw recovery from the humiliations and disasters of the American Revolution. Pitt reorganized the financial administration, established the new Sinking Fund, won a commercial treaty with France, and before England engaged in another war, raised her international prestige which had sunk so low before the American Revolution had ended. Pitt failed to carry parliamentary reform in 1785, and the agitation abated. But with the French Revolution, the spirits of the political reformers revived. The decade closed as it had opened, with liberals optimistic about the prospects for reform of the political system of England.

Price participated in some of these events. He supported the reform movement in the first part of the decade; in the middle years he aided in the establishment of the Sinking Fund and took interest in the making of the Constitution of the United States; after those labors he hoped to devote himself to private affairs. But the French Revolution drew him out of semiretirement to take part in his last great public cause.

In 1780 there was formed in England an organization for promoting parliamentary reform. The members adopted the name "The Society for Constitutional Information." However distasteful their ideas to the men who controlled the unreformed government of England, many members were socially and ancestrally unexceptionable. The society included eight peers of the realm, fifteen members of Parliament, and some solid middle class men such as Major John Cartwright, Dr.

John Jebb, John Horne Tooke, and Capel Lofft, who were already well known advocates of reform. Richard Price and his wealthy neighbor and parishioner, Thomas Rogers, also belonged to the society.

Price's pamphlets upon the American Revolution, without going into details, had criticized the narrowness of the suffrage and the unrepresentative character of Parliament. Unlike Major Cartwright, Price never attempted to work out a detailed agenda for reform, but he was in general a reformer. It is necessary to stress the word general because reformers in this period did not agree upon a specific program. This was the glaring weakness of the reform movement. The Society for Constitutional Information, for example, had no official program, and not all of its members desired universal manhood suffrage, for which a few like Price were calling. The reform question also concerned the Irish patriots. When some of them appealed to eminent English liberals for their opinions about reform in Ireland, the views of Price were solicited along with those of the Earl of Effingham, John Jebb, Major Cartwright, and the widely known Yorkshire clergyman, Christopher Wyvill. These men wrote letters published under the title *A Collection of the Letters which have been addressed to the volunteers of Ireland, on the subject of a parliamentary reform by the Earl of Effingham, Dr. Price . . .* (1783). The book attracted some attention; John Adams, who was not in London at the time, remembered it. In 1817 he wrote to James Madison concerning the question of suffrage, and he referred to the solicitation of the Irish volunteers. He said of Price, Jebb, and the Duke of Richmond, "These three great statesmen, divines, and philosophers solemnly advised a universal suffrage."[1]

When Pitt's moderate bill was defeated in Commons by a vote of 248-174, the reform agitation dwindled. Dr. Wyvill's Yorkshire Committee dissolved, the Society for Constitutional Information lapsed, and the reform spirit went into hiberna-

---

[1] Adrienne Koch and William Peden (eds.), *The Selected Writings of John Adams and John Quincy Adams* (New York, 1946), 201-202.

tion until the warming sun of the French revolutionary enthusiasm, which seemed to herald the dawn of a new political
era, drew it forth again.

In this period Price was associated with Dr. John Jebb,
and their friendship, which antedated the reform movement,
deepened. Not only on public affairs but also in their scientific interests they had a community of interest. On November
12, 1778, Price signed Jebb's certificate of nomination to the
Royal Society. Dr. Jebb, later converted to Unitarianism,
was an Anglican who thought highly of Price's religious
writings. Speaking of Price's essay on the meeting of virtuous
men in heaven, he said that Price had clearly demonstrated
his idea and "I do not know any consideration half so animating." In fact the doctrine as expounded by Price was so
attractive, he thought, as to convert a nonbeliever to Christianity.[2] He had as great regard for Price's political writings. Referring to his hopes for friendship between England and the
United States, he said he did not have to labor the point, for
"The great, the good Dr. Price has so ably touched this subject that it would be presumption in me to add any further
reflections of my own. To his sound and catholic doctrine,
I subscribe with all my heart."[3]

Price's friendship with Jebb showed how warm the personal
relations between Dissenters and Anglicans could be. Jebb
knew a good many Dissenters, judging from the number,
among them Price, who subscribed for his works.[4] Price belonged to a theological society in which Dissenters and Anglicans were drawn together by mutual respect for one another
as persons, and by common spiritual interests that transcended
sectarian limitations. The group, with the name "The Society
for promoting the Knowledge of the Scriptures," was organized in 1783. Theophilus Lindsey, John Disney, Andrew
Kippis, Joshua Toulmin, John Calder, Priestley, and Price
were all dissenting clergymen; Dr. Jebb, Bishop Edmund

[2] John Disney (ed.), *The Works Theological, Medical, Political, and Miscellaneous of John Jebb, M D., F.R.S.* (3 vols., London, 1787), II, 151-52.
[3] *Ibid.*, 485 n.   [4] *Ibid* , I, xxv.

Law of Carlisle, whose son Thomas married Martha Washington's granddaughter Betsy Custis, and John Newton, who was a member of the Clapham Sect, were Anglicans; and there were about thirty other members.[5] The rules confined the discussions to illustrations of Scripture, and the society encouraged nonsectarian publications. Though noble in purpose, the society did not flourish, and it disbanded after a few years. Yet to have been in the company of these men must have been stimulating to a person theologically inclined. Of three of the members, Thomas Belsham wrote, "What a proud preeminence to have enjoyed the intimacy of Price, of Priestley, and of Lindsey."[6]

In order to meet his London friends, Priestley had to journey from Birmingham, where he moved after leaving the service of Shelburne. Price and he wrote often to one another, and in the summer of 1784 Price visited his friend. He described the visit in a letter to Franklin, saying that Priestley's experiments were "going along successfully."[7] Not only was Price watching the scientific activities of others, but he was working upon experiments of his own. On May 23, 1783, he wrote to Emanuel Mendes da Costa, the fossilist and mineralogist, indicating his willingness to send certain mineral specimens da Costa had requested.[8]

Soon after, Price met a foreign visitor destined to become one of the famous men of the century. Mirabeau came to England bearing a letter of introduction from Franklin to Price, dated September 7, 1784.[9] He stayed in England for eight months, meeting in addition to Price such notables as Samuel Romilly, who translated his *Considerations on the Order of Cincinnatus*, Shelburne, the Duke of Richmond, and Edmund Burke.[10] He was in London when Price's *Observa-*

---

[5] Rutt, *Priestley*, I, 394-95 n.

[6] Lincoln, *English Dissent*, 60, quoting from Belsham's diary.

[7] Bigelow, *Franklin*, IX, 4.

[8] British Museum, Add. MSS., 28,541, F. 40

[9] W. C. Ford (comp.), *List of Benjamin Franklin Papers in the Library of Congress* (Washington, 1905), item 1390.

[10] Louis Barthou, *Mirabeau* (London, 1913), 111-12.

tions on the Importance of the American Revolution appeared. Since he was himself giving advice to Americans, he asked and received permission to summarize it in his *Considerations,* along with the letter of Turgot.

Amidst these activities Price still found time for his family. He continued his annual vacation in Wales, where he swam in the sea and visited relatives. But the tempo of his physical exertions was slowing. A fall from his horse in 1784 laid him up for several weeks and forced him to abandon riding. During this confinement he acceded to his physician's request to sit for his portrait to Benjamin West. One story had the physician demanding the sitting as a part of his fee. Price never fully recovered from the accident; pains in his back and legs occasionally brought misery.

Some of his relatives were with him in London. William Morgan, now a well known actuary, was happily married and the owner of a new house in the neighborhood of the Rothschilds. Morgan and Price often worked together upon actuarial problems. George Cadogan Morgan, who settled in London about 1786, opened a school at Southgate. He was interested in science, and through the good offices of Price, his paper called "Observations and Experiments on the Light of Bodies in a State of Combustion" was read before the Royal Society, with a postscript by Price intended to clarify the meaning of the term "phosphoric force."[11]

By this time Mrs. Price was seriously ill and almost entirely helpless. She was a care for Price, and he did his best to keep her amused. Often he played cards with her for an hour or two of an afternoon, and played cheerfully though he considered card playing a waste of time. Unlike many other Dissenters, he had no moral objections to card playing as such, but only the abuse of it. Mrs. Price, despite her affliction, was usually in good humor, and she was pleasant company for her husband and for friends who dropped in. During her last two years,

---

[11] *Philosophical Transactions,* LXXV (1785), part 1, pp. 190-212. This paper was read before Morgan came to London. The date of it was January 27, 1785.

however, her paralysis grew worse, so that reading and conversation were difficult. Out of consideration for her, Price chose to curtail his own activities. In 1784, for example, he turned down Shelburne's invitation to come to Bowood and renew his acquaintance with the Abbé Morellet. Shelburne understood, and did not press the matter out of respect for Mrs. Price. She died September 20, 1786, "after a long and tedious illness."[12] She was buried in the dissenting cemetery at Bunhill Fields, in the same grave with Price's Uncle Samuel. Price had been expecting her death for a long time, yet, as is always true in such circumstances, when the end came he was not prepared. He wrote soon after that it gave a "dreadful shock to my spirits; but I consider that the term of my survivorship cannot be long, and I look forward to a resurrection of all the virtuous to a better and endless life."[13] Because of the death of "the person who for near 30 years has divided with me the cares and pleasures of life," he desired "more than ever to retire from all public services."[14]

Price's friends offered solicitous advice during his despondency. Priestley assured him that time would restore his tranquillity, and to hasten recovery he urged him to travel away from London occasionally.[15] He also suggested a temporary retirement from the pulpit. Price had already given up his evening preaching at Newington Green, but he retained his pastorate at the Gravel-Pit in Hackney, nor did he follow Priestley's advice about taking a respite. He did, however, spend several weeks at the home of his nephew, and William and George Cadogan Morgan comforted him with their attentions.[16] Shelburne asked Price to come to Bowood Park in the country quiet of Wiltshire. There would be no other visitors for two months, and "We'll consider and treat you as a father," he promised.[17]

[12] Gentleman's Magazine, LVI (1786), part 2, p. 815.
[13] M.H.S.P. (1910), 626, Price to Willard, January 22, 1787.
[14] Price to Rush, January 26, 1787, Rush Manuscripts.
[15] Rutt, Priestley, I, 397-98, letter of October 23, 1786.
[16] Williams, A Welsh Family, 85.   [17] M.H.S.P. (1903), 351.

Though he declined the invitation, Price followed Shelburne's advice to keep busy. First, he rearranged his own affairs. His favorite sister, Mrs. Morgan, was happy to come from Wales and be his housekeeper. In London she could be near her sons. Then Price changed his residence, moving back to Hackney, after having lived in the quiet of Newington for nearly thirty years. His interests were in Hackney, where his meetinghouse stood. With these new arrangements and his varied interests, Price gained mental relief, but his physical ailments continued to bother him. To combat them he adhered to his strict regimen and continued to take his annual vacation. Thus, in the summer of 1787 he spent two months at East Bourne in Sussex, in "sea-bathing and dissipation," as he described it to Franklin.[18]

Writing to Franklin had always been one of Price's pleasures. When the war of the American Revolution ended they had resumed their correspondence about a variety of matters. For a year or two balloon ascensions were the rage on both sides of the Channel. Franklin sent an account of the one at Versailles in September, 1783, asking Price. to pass it on to the botanist Joseph Banks, then president of the Royal Society. With the letter came a small balloon that would rise when filled with "inflammable air," and a copy of Franklin's "A Letter to the Royal Society at Brussels," a witty, smutty burlesque of some scientific schemes. Two dissenting clergymen, Price and Priestley, chuckled over it. In telling Franklin of their amusement at his "Letter," Price described the split in the Royal Society caused by a faction opposing President Banks. The "Honest Whigs" were still meeting, and the members hoped Franklin would soon visit them. Franklin replied that some old ailments prevented his crossing the Channel at this time (August 16, 1784), but he warned Price not to be surprised if some Thursday he popped in to spend an "excellent evening" at the London Coffeehouse.

In the next March came Franklin's request for a list of books, to the value of £25, such as would inculcate sound prin-

18 Bigelow, *Franklin*, IX, 413.

ciples of religion and government. A town in Massachusetts had been named for Franklin, and the residents offered to build a steeple for the meetinghouse if he would furnish a bell. In his common sense fashion he suggested, instead of a bell, some books to be the nucleus of a local library. Would Price choose the books? Franklin's only direction was that Price should be certain to include his own writings. Price compiled the list, gave it to Franklin's nephew for transmission, and donated some of his own works.

Soon afterwards Franklin crossed the Atlantic for the last time, after putting in briefly at Southampton. Price wrote on November 5, 1785, of his regret at having been unable to join those who journeyed down to see Franklin off. Would Franklin convey his thanks to the Philosophical Society of Philadelphia for electing him a member? Benjamin Vaughan had just brought his diploma. Two years later Franklin procured membership for Price in the Pennsylvania Society for Abolishing Negro Slavery, of which Franklin was president. Price accepted the membership gratefully, while modestly admitting there was little he could do beyond wishing the society success in its endeavors.

One of the tasks Price undertook after the death of his wife was the preparation of a new edition of his work on morals, now thirty years old. Shelburne encouraged him.[19] Though his fame was established by having helped in the creation of the Sinking Fund, Shelburne thought Price should be remembered above all for his work on morality, by which "you will leave some still better legacy to mankind." Price worked steadily and the new edition, the third, appeared in 1787, somewhat revised, and enlarged by the addition of "A Dissertation on the Being and Attributes of the Deity."

Shelburne's advice to Price was sometimes inconsistent. Only two months after urging him to let his fame rest upon his work in morals, Shelburne asked Price to devote his attention to the cause of international peace.[20] It happened that at the time Price was not only revising his book on morals

[19]M H.S.P. (1903), 351, September 29, 1786.   [20] Ibid , 360

but was also preparing a collection of his sermons for publication. Facetiously, Shelburne pointed out how fruitless it
was for Price to devote so much time to theology. After all,
most men agreed about the existence of God and the nature
of His attributes. Would it not be better if Price tried to improve a world in which peace was so precarious? So, though
he would "read your Sermons I am sure with great pleasure, . . .
I want you to live hereafter with the Turgots and the Neckers,
and to leave the Doct^rs and the Archdeacons to dye by the
hands of one another."

Price smiled and went ahead. Though he was a clergyman,
he had published comparatively little about theology. Besides,
his friends had urged and his congregation petitioned him to
undertake the project.[21] His progress was languid. After all,
he told Rush, he was not a Franklin who, at eighty, had such
wonderful vigor.[22] And a theological subject, beset with sub-
tleties, required careful handling. A political pamphlet, struck
off in the heat of agitated times, could be turned out quickly,
but not a treatise on religion. Priestley, himself a rapid, even
hasty, worker, was impatient at Price's slowness. On July 4,
1786, he told the Reverend Joseph Bretland that he had no
idea when the book would be finished, for Price "is slow in all
his proceedings."[23] Nevertheless, the book was nearly ready
by November, and Price's friends were awaiting its publication. Samuel Vaughan, then living in Philadelphia, wrote on
November 4 of his anticipation about the forthcoming book,
and three weeks later Shelburne said he intended to read it.[24]

Published soon afterward, the book was well received. It
was reissued in Philadelphia in 1788 and in Boston in 1794
and 1815. It evoked some replies despite the Advertisement to
the reader, dated November 24, in which Price stated that
"being determined not to engage in Controversy, I shall make
no reply to any Animadversions on the account which . . . I
have given of the Doctrines of Christianity." Priestley warned
Price on January 7, 1787, that like it or not, some Socinians

21 Price to Rush, July 30, 1786, Rush Manuscripts.   22 *Ibid.*
23 Rutt, *Priestley,* I, 391.   24 M.H.S.P. (1903), 355, 360.

would attempt to refute him. Among these was Priestley himself, always ready to take up the pen. He not only made some objections to Price's ideas in private correspondence, but informed Price that he intended to include a rebuttal in his *Defences of Unitarianism for the year 1786*, which he did. Priestley's was friendly opposition, for, as he wrote to Belsham, he and Price "agree in thinking, that a Christian spirit is of more value than even Christian truth."[25] Priestley also had a letter to Price in his *Defences . . . for the year 1787*. Price had to take notice of Priestley's remarks, and so he brought out a second edition in 1787 which contained an appendix replying to Priestley.

The book was entitled *Sermons on the Christian Doctrine as received by the Different Denominations of Christians. To which are added, Sermons on the Security and Happiness of a Virtuous Course, on the Goodness of God, and the Resurrection of Lazarus*. The latter sermons were moral rather than doctrinal. The controversial part was the discussion of the theological distinctions among various Christian denominations.

Price began by pointing out wherein Christians agreed. All denominations accepted the Gospel teachings of one living, true, and perfect God whom mankind should serve. None denied that repentance and holy living pleased God, who rewarded and punished men after judging them according to their works. Despite a variety of beliefs about the nature and powers of Christ, all Christians held that Christ was sent of God and was the true Messiah who worked miracles, suffered on the Cross, died, arose from the tomb, and would come a second time. The differences among Christians were therefore trivial, since Christ is the Resurrection and the Life. Whether Christ was human or divine was not important, for under either connotation He was man's salvation.

Nevertheless Christians disagreed, often bitterly, and Price tried to discuss dispassionately the doctrines of Trinitarians and Calvinists on the one side and Unitarians (Arians) and

[25] Rutt, *Priestley*, II, 521 n., letter of March 9, 1787.

Socinians on the other. His method was descriptive rather than analytical. He took up four main problems: the nature of Diety; original sin; the nature of Christ; and the role of Christ concerning salvation. The first two were quickly disposed of. Arians and Socinians denied the Trinity and rejected the idea of original sin. The doctrine of inherent depravity, insisted Price, was incompatible with freedom of will.

On the other two points, Price parted company with the Socinians as well as the Calvinists and their doctrine of Christ purchasing, through His death, salvation for the elect. To the Socinian, Christ was merely a man who died to induce us to be reconciled to God, not by paying the price of His life for ours, but by bringing truth and virtue to us. The Arian believed in the pre-existent dignity of Christ who, though not divine, was the Author and the means of immortality. Concerning the nature of Christ, Arianism stood between orthodox Trinitarianism and Socinianism. Price confessed his inability to say precisely what degree of superiority to mortal men Christ possessed. In the process of salvation, Christ did more than convey God's mercy, as the Socinians would have it. Through His own benevolence as a Saviour He helped men attain salvation. In the end, however, men had to make their will and actions concur with the plan of God, for the exercise of free will was a part of the grand design of salvation.

It was this section of the book that elicited criticisms. Neither the Trinitarians nor the Socinians accepted the Arian conception of the person and nature of Christ. Priestley's replies dwelt largely upon this matter. The Arians found themselves in the embarrassing position of any center party attacked from the extremities. Price remained until his death firm in his Arian creed, but the history of his sect in the eighteenth century revealed a constant migration of Arians into the ranks of Socinians. The Arian theology was difficult to explain in precise terms, there being in it some vagueness about the nature of Christ. It was much easier to consider Christ either as both human and divine, or as only human.

The Arian wanted to do a little of both, without admitting either conception. His definition of Christ was not at all clear.

The last five sermons were sincere homilies which all Christians could accept. They were written in the optimistic, sweet, and benevolent manner characteristic of Price's morality. The sermon on the security of a virtuous course could appeal even to nonbelievers; it contained the same argument from chance that Price had used thirty years earlier. Being entirely practical, Price repeated another thought found in his book on morals, that virtue was rewarded in this life as well as in the next. The sermon on the happiness of a virtuous course continued this theme. The sermons on the goodness of God followed two lines of reasoning. The first employed the Thomistic argument from the definition of the nature of God. The second showed that God's goodness was to be seen in His works, in nature, and in His giving us the Gospel and sending Christ to save us. The last sermon, on the resurrection of Lazarus, was the one Priestley especially liked. The raising of Lazarus assured us that the Divine mission of Christ was to raise all mankind from death.

Whatever his readers thought of Price's views, many of them said they enjoyed the book. Franklin read with "great pleasure" the sermons which Price sent him as a gift. Shelburne was "delighted" by them, and he thought the first one, concerning the agreements among the Christians, ought to be taught in every school in England. Children might well learn to spell out of this sermon, he said. It and the one on the happiness of a virtuous course were Shelburne's favorites. He called Price's sentiments truly Christian, and in the rest of a long letter he deplored the bickering among Christian denominations.[26] Benjamin Rush, who received a copy from Bishop White, praised the moderation of Price's discourses. He even went to the trouble of copying out passages for a correspondent who lived in another state. From Crishna Nagar in India came a letter of appreciation from Sir William Jones, the famous orientalist, judge of the high court in Calcutta,

[26] M.H.S.P. (1903), 362-64.

and husband of Anna Maria Shipley, the daughter of Price's good friend the Bishop of St. Asaph.[27] Theophilus Lindsey read the sermons critically, and told Price he detected a similarity with the views of Bishop Butler on the nature and dignity of Christ. Price had been a student of Butler's writings since his schooldays; in fact, he sat for his portrait to West with a copy of the *Analogy* in his hand. He denied, however, the validity of Lindsey's remark, especially because he did not hold to the worship of Christ, as did Butler. In a letter of May 14, 1790, Price answered other points Lindsey raised, affirming that unlike the Socinians, he was "unconvinced of the doctrine of the simple humanity of Christ."[28]

The reviewer for the *Gentleman's Magazine* was unkind.[29] Calling these sermons Price's "dying creed," he wondered, irrelevantly, whether the members of Price's congregation could follow him in all these subtle distinctions among the views of Christian denominations. Turning from the understanding of the spoken to the written word, the reviewer accused Price of oversimplifying. It is difficult to see just what the reviewer would have wanted Price to do. A few months later the same magazine mentioned the second edition of the sermons with Price's appendix containing Priestley's criticisms.[30]

No more than the reviewer for the *Gentleman's Magazine* could Price satisfy an elderly lady who thought he was much too magnanimous towards Priestley.[31] Many people held Priestley in disrepute for his aggressive Socinianism; even Shelburne branded his former librarian as an atheist and an enemy to religion.[32] The old woman said she had always been taught to look up to Price as a defender of the Christian faith, but she was displeased that he had let pass so lightly his friend Priestley's efforts to destroy Christianity. If you would fight,

---

[27] Morgan, *Price*, 115 n. Jones was also a friend of the Abbé Morellet.
[28] *Ibid.*, 111 n., 112.   [29] Vol. LVII (1787), part 1, p. 158.
[30] *Ibid.*, part 2, p. 807.
[31] *Ibid.*, LVIII (1788), part 1, p. 193, for the letter of this complainant.
[32] M.H.S P. (1903), 363.

she said, "fight the good fight of faith," and please be more careful whom you choose as friends. Such cavils no longer bothered Price. He was accustomed to criticisms of his writings; as to his personal conduct, a clergyman had to be philosophical about admonitions.

If Dissenters of different sects quarreled about theology, they agreed upon one matter, the importance of education for the young. Price thought "Nothing, certainly, can be of more importance."[33] Dissenters were rightly proud of their academies, which were the best schools in England, and they gave generously and worked hard for their establishment and support. Despite the dissenting emphasis upon education, for various reasons the history of the academies was a checkered one. Some schools had long terms of existence, while others only briefly manifested the fleeting hopes of ambitious founders.

Late in 1785 some of the independent London Dissenters became alarmed at the recent closings of their academies at Exeter, Warrington, and Hoxton. The one at Daventry being insufficient, they decided to found a new academy at Hackney, after a committee had failed to elicit the support of the Coward trustees for the reopening of the Hoxton institution. The chairman of the committee was Thomas Rogers, and among other original members were Price, the Reverend Hugh Worthington, and Benjamin Vaughan.[34] The committee asked the trustees of the defunct Warrington academy for the use of the institution's library and "Apparatus," a request that was partially granted. In the meantime the committee, having received assurances of support for the Hackney project, drew up a prospectus.[35] At the March 10 meeting, the chairman requested that formal invitations to serve as tutors be proferred Price, Kippis, Worthington, and Abraham Rees. When the fund raising drive began, subscriptions came in quickly.[36]

[33] Price to Rush, July 30, 1786, Rush Manuscripts.

[34] Andrew Kippis, A Sermon Preached at the Old Jewry . . . on occasion of a New Academical Institution, among Protestant Dissenters . . . (London, 1786), 57-58.

[35] Ibid., 63-65.   [36] Ibid., 70-72.

On April 26, 1786, Kippis, preaching to the school's supporters, revealed the purposes and hopes of the founders. By teaching obedience to God and to their parents and by imparting a knowledge of religion, the college would train its students for life on earth and in heaven.[37] More specifically, the college had to prepare young men for their professional careers, at the same time molding them into good citizens by inspiring in them noble sentiments of liberty. Therefore, students should take part in politics. The curriculum would embrace the sciences and literature as well as divinity, in order to serve students' inclinations for either the ministry or lay careers. The founders preferred to call the institution a "college," for "The word Academy," said Worthington, "does not convey a proper idea of our plan of education."[38]

Price decided to accept a tutorship in the college, though Priestley tried to discourage him.[39] Priestley, who had taught in the old Warrington academy, knew how taxing teaching really was. He thought an occasional discourse from Price would have an excellent effect, however, and to lecture only now and then would be more in keeping with Price's dignity, since he could choose his own topics. Shelburne also offered advice about school administration.[40] He preferred more emphasis upon modern languages, and he suggested shorter vacation periods than were customary.

Upon the formal opening of the college, which had been delayed several months, Dr. Richard Price preached the sermon. It was published as *The Evidence for a future Period of Improvement in the State of Mankind, with the Means and Duty of Improving It, represented in a Discourse delivered on Wednesday the 25th of April, 1787, at the Meeting-House in the Old Jewry, London, to the Supporters of a New Academical Institution Among Protestant Dissenters.* In this sermon Price expounded his long run optimism and

---

[37] *Ibid.,* 8.

[38] McLachlan, *English Education,* 246, quoting Worthington's sermon of May 6, 1789.

[39] Rutt, *Priestley,* I, 396-97, letter of October 23, 1786.

[40] M.H.S.P. (1903), 359, letter of November 29, 1786.

that of the eighteenth century in the inexorable progress and
the inevitable perfection of mankind. By the time of Christ's
second coming, the Christian faith would have attained universal acceptance, and morality, based on Christian principles, would reign. Even in Price's own day there was evidence of "a progressive improvement in human affairs which
will terminate in greater degrees of light and virtue and happiness than have been yet known."[41]

The teachings of Scripture, history, and reason supported
this belief. After citing many Biblical passages, Price made
history show that as a result of many changes "there is the
same difference between the state of our species now and
its state at first, as there is between a youth approaching to
manhood and a child just born."[42] Progress sometimes came
in cycles, but no real gain was ever wholly lost. Thus, "there
may come a time when *every* country will be what *many* are
now; and when *some* will be advanced to a state much
higher."[43] The history of natural philosophy illustrated this
teaching. Contemporary experience also demonstrated the
reality of human progress and the bright promise for the
future. The advances in philosophical (scientific) knowledge
since Newton's time, the appearance of "more enlarged views
and liberal sentiments in religion" leading toward "universal
toleration," the acceptance of "juster notions also of the origins
and end of civil government," the growth of the conviction
"that all encroachments on the rights of conscience are pernicious and impious," the spread of humanitarianism and the
mounting opposition to warfare as a foolish and sinful activity, the growing interdependence of the world, the diffusion
of knowledge—all these revealed man as "a milder animal than
he was and the world outgrowing its evils, superstitions giving
way, antichrist falling, and the Millenium hastening."[44]

If human progress was to continue, each generation had
to do its part in the advance of mankind towards perfection.
Price's enlightened generation enjoyed unusual opportunities

[41] *Evidence for Improvement*, 5.   [42] *Ibid.*, 12.   [43] *Ibid.*, 13.
[44] *Ibid.*, 25.

for enlarging civil liberties by everywhere securing freedom of
speech, press, and religion. Besides disestablishing state
churches, men had to recognize "That nothing is very important except an honest mind; nothing fundamental except
religious practice, and a sincere desire to know and do the
will of God."[45] Progress also demanded the reform of political
institutions, for the actions of governments always impinged
upon human happiness. England, of course, needed to reform
her Parliament, which did not require the overthrow of the
inherited constitution. Here Price defended the Dissenters,
who were so prominent in the movements for political reform,
and who so often had been the objects of malicious and false
accusations. Price knew no Dissenters who wanted to change
"our mixed form of government," which was good "in theory,"
into a "Democracy," that is, a government whose legislative
branch was all powerful. Separation of powers and checks and
balances were desirable. Having spoken of specific political
problems, Price summed up his political creed, relating it to
his moral philosophy. Despotic governments were "debasing";
"Free governments, on the contrary, exalt the human character."[46]

The real theme of Price's discourse was the dependence of
progress upon education. Among their duties, schools must
teach youth morality, learning, zeal, and piety, "from a regard
to the moral government of the Diety and a future judgment."[47]
Price wanted the Hackney College to follow these precepts
rather than emulate schools that imparted only "learning
which puffs up." Bigoted erudition stuffed the mind with
prejudice and darkened rather than enlightened the world.
The best type of education taught love of virtue and benevolence; protected a student against dogmatism by revealing
the fallibility of the understanding; and trained him to be
"attentive to evidence." Hackney College must turn out not
only competent scholars, but "good men, upright citizens,
and *honest* and *candid* believers."[48] These aims were attain-

[45] *Ibid.*, 38.   [46] *Ibid.*, 29.   [47] *Ibid.*, 38.   [48] *Ibid.*, 45

able-if freedom of teaching and research prevailed in the institution, for "Free enquiry can be hostile to nothing but absurdity and bigotry."[49] Price believed deeply that one of the conditions of a free society was an educated citizenry. The improvement of mankind would be assured by men who used to their utmost the powers given to them by Providence.

With this inspiration the college began instruction in a room in Dr. Williams' library, in Cripplegate. Of the six students, all but one were candidates for the ministry. By the spring of 1790 forty-nine were enrolled and housed in the recently acquired college building. The curriculum included ancient languages, divinity studies, sciences, and politics. Ministerial students took two years of advanced work beyond the three year course.[50] When instruction began, there were only four tutors for this ambitious curriculum. There was considerable latitude. Price taught, not formal courses, but in the general fields of mathematics, with emphasis upon Newton's *Principia* and life annuities. He also lectured upon morals. Thomas Broadhurst, who studied under him, left his recollections of Price as a teacher.[51] George Morgan accompanied Price to class, to assist him if needed. Later he succeeded his uncle as a tutor in the college. Price had only three students, as they were the only ones of the small beginning enrollment far enough advanced to go along with his lectures "on Jebb's *Excerpta,* Newton's *Principia* and Dr. Thomas Simpson's *Treatise on Fluxions.*" He did not lecture formally, but conducted his class as a discussion group centering its attention upon philosophy and politics. With his defects as a public speaker he would not have been an effective classroom lecturer, though meeting a few advanced students in informal fashion, he may well have been a stimulating teacher.

[49] *Ibid.,* 46.

[50] Thomas Belsham, *The Importance of Truth, and the Duty of making an open profession of it* (London, 1790), 50.

[51] McLachlan, *English Education,* 248.

Price taught in the college for only a few months. His colleagues were not entirely satisfied with his work; perhaps they thought that he was not carrying his full share of the burden. Apart from this, Price found the work too strenuous. He had reluctantly accepted the post because London friends thought his connection would add prestige to the school and because he believed he had a duty to perform.[52] But he was in frail health, and he was not up to the physical effort required of him. In the autumn of 1787 he resigned, though he continued to take an interest in the affairs of the college, and he remembered it in his will.

Hackney College never fulfilled the hopes of its founders. Its troubles were not exclusively financial. During the excitement of the early days of the French Revolution, faculty and students alike became active in the revived reform movement. Burke called the college a "hot bed of sedition." Ten members of the committee that had organized the college were members of the Revolution Society, and of these ten, Price, Kippis, and Rees were on the original faculty.[53] The college was even so bold, and tactless, as to entertain Tom Paine at a dinner. Priestley's connection with the institution after July, 1791, did not increase its respectability in the estimation of conservatives. In fact, the Birmingham riot, during which Priestley's home and laboratory were burned, was touched off, in part, by a pamphlet written by a Hackney student and circulated in Birmingham.[54] The students evidently took their political lessons seriously. The increasing severity of governmental suppression of reform activities brought trouble for the college. The deaths of Price,, of Thomas Rogers in 1793, and of Kippis two years later caused even Dissenters to lose confidence in the school. Former contributors, who had already sunk £20,000 in the academic venture, refused to support it any longer, and the college closed in the summer of 1796. But there were men who mourned the passing of the school and

[52] M.H.S.P. (1910), 627, letter to Joseph Willard, October 10, 1787.
[53] Lincoln, *English Dissent*, 97, n. 1.
[54] McLachlan, *English Education*, 252.

of the hopes it symbolized. Thomas Belsham, who joined the faculty in 1789, pronounced its valedictory: "The spirit of the times was against it."[55]

Regardless of his professions about wanting to retire from public affairs, Price was drawn into them in spite of himself, and probably not as reluctantly as he tried to make himself believe. Early in 1787 the Reverend John Acland, an Anglican clergyman, revived the old project for friendly societies with the publication of a pamphlet entitled *A Plan for rendering the Poor Independent on Public Contribution . . . To Which is added, a Letter from Dr. Price, containing his sentiments and calculations on the Subject.* Price approved of the principle of friendly societies, but he found defects in Acland's calculations. At Acland's request he suggested an actuarially sound plan which would provide poor relief, encourage frugality and industry among the poor, promote the growth of population, and remove evils in the existing poor laws. He wished for Acland greater success "than Baron *Maseres* and myself met with some years ago." Acland modified his scheme, hoping that if he could demonstrate the soundness of the principle, Parliament would work out a detailed plan. A Lord Stair or a Dr. Price would be needed to make the precise calculations.[56]

Price did not want to devote any time to working for the plan, but he was willing to assist if asked. A bill containing a scheme similar to Acland's failed in 1787.[57] Two years later the idea was revived; Price computed tables for the select committee; but the Lords, as in 1773, defeated the project.[58] Parliament finally passed in 1793 an act for encouraging friendly societies. Under this and similar laws the friendly society movement became during the nineteenth century an important feature of the self-help activities of the working class. When, just before the first World War, a national system of old-age pensions and sickness and unemployment insurance was estab-

---

[55] *Ibid.,* 254.   [56] *A Plan,* 7.

[57] *Parl. Hist.,* XXVI, 1059-62; *Commons Journals,* XLII, 703, 714, 730, 786.

[58] Thomas, *Price,* 59; *Commons Journals,* XLIV, 212, 276, 288, 370, 433, 441.

lished, the friendly societies did not cease operations but merged their programs in the new one set up by Parliament. The time of Price was linked to the time of Lloyd George, another Welshman, by the continuous history of the friendly societies. It would be too strong a statement to say that Price was the father of the old-age pension system.[59] Nevertheless, he had a place in the friendly society movement. The publicity given to his calculations concerning friendly society schemes saved some of these associations from failure and enabled others to establish themselves upon a basis as sound as the actuarial knowledge attained in Price's time could make them.[60]

Had there been nothing else, Price's heavy correspondence would have kept him busy. His numerous friends were still keeping in touch with him, and often seeking his aid or advice. For example, Benjamin Rush wrote in behalf of the Reverend Elhaman Winchester, who was moving to London after having founded a Universalist church in Philadelphia. Winchester wanted a letter from Rush introducing him to Price, "for Americans of every profession and mark expect to find a friend in the friend of human kind."[61]

Then there was the affair with Joel Barlow, the self-appointed apostle of the gospel of the rights of man. He came to Europe in 1788 on the business of a land company and remained to participate in the revolutionary upheavals of the 1790's. The acquaintance of Price with Barlow began in 1786 when Barlow sent Price the manuscript of his *The Vision of Columbus* and asked him to find a publisher for it. Why Barlow sought Price's assistance may be explained, perhaps, by the quotation from Rush's letter. Price, an innocent party, worried about the business. He asked Thomas Day, the author of *The History of Sanford and Merton* and an advocate of Rousseauism and humanitarian reforms, to advise him. Even before reading the epic, Day had some opinions about it.[62]

---

[59] As does Thomas, *Price*, 60.

[60] Price's plans were discussed thoroughly and favorably by Eden, *The State of the Poor*, I, 373-80, 616-17 n.

[61] M.H.S.P. (1903), 369, letter of July 29, 1787.   [62] *Ibid.*, 339-41.

He doubted if the poem had any merit, for he had not seen any of American origin that did. If it was published and not cordially received, Barlow might be angry, for he belonged apparently to the "genus irritable vatum." Barlow might take offense for another reason. "When it is remembered that Milton sold his immortal work for ten pound, what offer of a London bookseller for this production of Western genius is likely to satisfy the author?" Day suggested that Price simply tell Barlow what publication possibilities existed, leaving the author to decide how best to dispose of his "invaluable property." Above all, Day warned Price not to underwrite the publication, for he would surely lose money.

Price took Day's advice. In a tactful letter to Barlow he suggested that because of the praise of the armies of France and America and the censures of England to be found in *The Vision,* the poem was "improper to be published in this country."[63] So Price recommended publication in America or Paris, and tried to make Barlow feel good by saying the poem would be a credit both to its author and his country. *The Vision* was published in Hartford in 1787. Barlow must not have been displeased with Price, for he turned up in London bearing a letter of introduction from Jefferson, dated February 7, 1788.[64] Jefferson was sure Price would be glad to see Barlow and show him around London, because he knew that Price had read *The Vision* in manuscript and had expressed admiration for it. Barlow spent only a short time in London on this trip, but Europe would see and hear much of him during the next several years.

Price's association with another American was of quite a different character. John Adams was minister to the court of St. James from 1785 to 1788. Writing to Jefferson many years later, Adams revealed, "I was intimate with Dr. Price. I had much conversation with him at his own house, at my house,

[63] Joel Barlow Papers, Box 2, Harvard Library. A summary of this letter was furnished me by Professor Merrill Jensen of the University of Wisconsin.

[64] *The Writings of Thomas Jefferson* (20 vols., Washington, 1903-1904), VI, 424.

and at the houses and tables of my friends."[65] The sentiments
in this letter agreed with those Adams expressed to Price only
a year after returning to the United States. "There are few
portions of my life that I recollect with more satisfaction than
the hours I spent at Hackney, under your ministry, and in
private society, and conversation with you at other places."[66]
Beyond doubt, much of their talk concerned political subjects,
ideas of democracy and liberty, and the future of the United
States. Adams arrived in England when Price's *Observations
on the Importance of the American Revolution* was fresh, and
it was the publication by Price, in this work, of Turgot's letter
of 1778 that helped prompt him to write his *Defence of the
Constitutions*. . . . Price read the book as soon as it came
out in London, the first volume having been given to him by
Adams early in 1787. He told Adams he thought the book
would do some good in the United States, which indeed it did,
for it was available during the summer the Constitutional Convention was sitting in Philadelphia. Adams was grateful for
Price's kind opinion. It had been his desire to produce a work
for the instruction of young people, "which would be worthy
of the pen and talents of a Hume, a Gibbon, a Price and a
Priestley."[67] In order to appreciate this remark, one must remember that whatever else he may have been, Adams was not
a sycophant.

Price, who admired Adams' "abilities and character," revealed his sorrow over Adams' departure in a letter of March
24, 1788.[68] This letter, to an unnamed correspondent, also
indicated some of Price's activities and interests at the time.
Price assured this person that he carried out his commission
in passing on to Shelburne and Colonel Barré the letter intended for them. Both of these gentlemen were active in opposing some amendments to the India Act of 1784. It would

[65] *Ibid.*, XIII, 372-73, letter of September 14, 1813.
[66] Adams (ed), *Works of John Adams*, IX, 558, letter of May 20, 1789.
[67] M H.S.P. (1903), 364-65, letter of February 4, 1787.
[68] Manuscript in the R. B. Adam Collection. Robert F. Metzdorf, curator
of the Adam Collection when it was at the University of Rochester Library,
Rochester, New York, provided me with a photostat of this letter.

be dangerous, thought Price, to enlarge the powers of the Board of Control for India. To do so would be to threaten the constitution as much as did the ill-fated bill of 1783, which would have lodged power "not in the King but in an aristocracy that created a kind of 4th estate in the Kingdom." The opposition was unsuccessful, and "I am afraid it always will be so when it contradicts the views of the crown, in consequence of the miserable inadequateness of our representation." Price hoped "you will do better in America." Finally he apologized for writing so hastily, but he was pressed by "more engagements than a person so slow and so easily encumbered as myself can properly attend to."

Some of these "engagements" were with his old friend John Howard. Price saw much of Howard when he was in England between tours of the European lazarettos. When Howard was away, they wrote regularly to one another. In the late 1780's, some of Howard's admirers undertook a subscription for a statue of him. Howard, shocked, protested indignantly. Price, with others who knew Howard's character better than the well meaning campaigners, disapproved of the project vehemently enough to stifle it. Only after Howard's death was a memorial erected.

In the summer of 1789 Howard left on his last journey which was to take him to Russia and, he intended, to Constantinople again. He was past sixty, he was not strong, and his prison visits exposed him to many dangers. Price was a few years older than Howard and in even more delicate health. Consequently, both men had a premonition that they might never meet again. In the sentimental fashion of the time, they "took a most affectionate and pathetic leave of one another . . . and their farewell corresponded with the solemnity of such an occasion."[69]

Price was past his middle sixties, and the tribulations of old age were increasing. To the despondency brought on by his own decline were added the sorrows caused by the deaths and infirmities of former associates. Dr. Adams, master of Pem-

69 Aikin, *Life of Howard*, 118.

broke College, Oxford, a friend since Price's early manhood, wrote in October, 1788, that his life was drawing to a close, and he hoped in the next world to continue his friendship with Price. In this same month Price had the unpleasant duty of enclosing in his letter to Franklin one written by Kitty Shipley telling of the death of her father, their old friend Bishop Shipley of St. Asaph. Franklin was also failing. He was trying hard to complete his autobiography and sent as much as he had done to Price in manuscript. In one of his last letters to Price, May 31, 1789, Franklin commented on the deaths of Shipley and other mutual friends.[70] He was still the same old Franklin, as intellectually curious as ever. He sent Price two volumes of the transactions of the American Philosophical Society, asking him, if he already owned them, to send these two on to the Duke de la Rochefoucauld.

Price himself could no longer avoid reflecting upon death, and he took comfort in looking toward the meeting with old friends in a "better country." Franklin had said in one of his last letters that as a person grew older, he was furnished with helps to wean him from this life, and the loss of old friends whom he would meet in the hereafter was one of these.

So it seemed that the old order was passing, and Price was prepared to pass with it and join his friends of other years in Heaven. But he lived long enough to see the old order give way to a new one that would, he was sure, bring happiness and peace for mankind. He was, as it turned out, more than a witness of the stirring early events of the French Revolution; he took an active part in this cause which, his last, he thought was his greatest. For a moment despondency gave way to animation and optimism. Physical infirmities were forgotten. Almost youthfully vigorous again, Price helped usher in the new era with all of the enthusiasm he had displayed in earlier times.

[70] Bigelow, *Franklin*, X, 85-86.

CHAPTER XIII

THE FRENCH REVOLUTION

WORDSWORTH expressed the rapture felt by many people in the early months of the French Revolution. Recalling his youthful aspirations, he wrote years later in his autobiographical poem, *The Prelude,*

> Bliss was it in that dawn to be alive,
> But to be young was very Heaven![1]

More soberly, but just as optimistically, men in England who for twenty years had hoped for political reforms sympathized with the efforts of the French to end despotism and to limit the powers of their king by a constitution that would secure for the people a voice in political affairs and guarantee their rights as men.

In its earliest stages the French Revolution excited no alarm in England, and in fact no widespread interest until the fall of the Bastille. Thereafter the survivors of the earlier reform movements in England stirred themselves. They discerned a connection between what was happening in France and what they thought needed to be done in England. If the French could reform their corrupt old regime and bring the government under the control of the sovereign people, why could not the English, whose constitution was already formed? The idea of reviving the reform agitation caught hold rapidly, and by the autumn of 1789 reformers were active once again. Dr. Price was one of the most enthusiastic of all, and it was with his sermon, as the saying goes, that the French Revolution in England began.

[1] Book XI, lines 108-109.

The changes in France had not come unheralded. For two years before the Estates-General assembled in May, 1789, there had been unusual doings in the provinces and in the capital. Price saw portents in them. As early as September 26, 1787, he told Franklin that he saw a new spirit in Europe, especially in Holland, Brabant, and France.[2] That spirit, he said, originated in America and was spreading abroad. The prospect of a better ordering of affairs in the United States encouraged the spread of liberal ideas throughout the world. Because of the war between England and America and because of the writings of wise men explaining the true principles of government, "the minds of men are becoming more enlightened, and the silly despots of the world are likely to be forced to respect human rights, and to take care not to govern too much, lest they should not govern at all."

In view of all this, the 1788 meeting of the Revolution Society had special significance. This organization commemorated every November 4 the birthday of William III and, of course, the Revolution of 1688. Price, with so many of the Dissenters, belonged to the Revolution Society. As a distinguished advocate of the rights of men, he was invited to deliver the sermon to the society, but he declined because of ill health. Along with four hundred others, however, he attended the dinner. He proposed, as one of the forty-one toasts, "The memory of the Bishops who were imprisoned in the Tower, and may all clerical men show themselves equal enemies to arbitrary power."[3] The celebrants that night could hardly avoid thinking of events in France.

Price looked eagerly for news from France, more so than ever during the winter preceding the meeting of the Estates-General. One of his best sources of information was Thomas Jefferson, the kindred spirit who was American minister to France. Jefferson's letters to Price reflected his confidence that the changes in France were for the better. In a letter of January 8, 1789, he described the preparations for the assembling of the Estates-General. On May 19, he was certain that

2 Bigelow, *Franklin*, IX, 411-14.   3 Quoted in Thomas, *Price*, 124.

a good constitutional system would be worked out. Two days before the fall of the Bastille, he predicted "the beginning of the reformation of the governments of Europe."[4] Jefferson's messages strengthened Price's hopes for the coming of a better world, of which they had talked in London in 1786.

Other correspondents corroborated Jefferson's views. Two liberal Frenchmen, the Duke de la Rochefoucauld and Rabaut St. Etienne, sent news and opinions to Price. In the summer of 1789 his nephew, George Cadogan Morgan, traveled in France and found evidence to support his sympathy for the aims of the Revolutionaries. He called on Jefferson on July 13, and next day he saw the Bastille fall. Like other liberals, he took that event to mean the destruction of the symbol of tyranny. His letters, describing the miseries of the French peasantry, also expressed the aspirations of the Revolutionaries. From Paris he went on to Dijon, Lyons, Marseilles, Italy, Switzerland, Germany, and Holland.[5] Everywhere he felt the beneficent effects of the revolution. By September, when he returned to England, he believed that the revolution was nearly over. With soaring spirits Price listened to Morgan's glowing accounts of what he had seen in France.

During the late summer of 1789 Price went to Wales for his vacation. The rest and the sea-bathing refreshed him; he returned to London feeling better than he had for several years. But something else had renewed his vigor and animation—the events in France, the belief that a new era had arrived. Though his physical condition was not fundamentally altered, mental exhilaration diminished the old pains in his back and legs.

When November 4 came around again, Price accepted without hesitation the invitation to address the Society for Commemorating the Revolution in Great Britain. The celebration of 1789 was the greatest of all, for it had international, even universal, meaning. Price made the most of the occasion.

This was a busy, feverish, memorable day in Price's life. At the Old Jewry Chapel he delivered his celebrated sermon.

---

[4] M.H S.P. (1903), 373-74.   [5] Williams, A Welsh Family, 100-11.

In the enthusiastic audience were many of his old dissenting friends, as well as his nephew William Morgan, Henry Beaufoy, M.P., a constant champion in Parliament of the efforts to repeal the Test and Corporation Acts, Earl Stanhope, and four dukes—Richmond, Norfolk, Leeds, and Manchester. Price's sermon was long, and he delivered it so ardently and eloquently, though feeling some bodily pain, that even the intoxication of the excitement of his audience could not allay his exhaustion. After this oratorical triumph, probably the greatest in his long career, he had to go home to bed. By evening he felt better, and he was able to attend the dinner of the society at the London Tavern. William Godwin noted in his diary that he dined with "the Revolutionists," among them Kippis, Rees, Towers, Lindsey, Disney, and Belsham—all dissenting clergymen—and the young Samuel Rogers.[6] Numerous toasts prolonged the dinner. Again Price was the animating spirit. He moved the congratulatory address that was unanimously adopted and sent to the National Assembly of France. So Price, twice on the same day, expressed himself upon the revolutions in England and France. In doing so, he helped raise a storm of controversy. It swept England for three years and kept the printing presses busy turning out pamphlets written to support or refute the reforming ideas Price and others advanced.

Price called his sermon *A Discourse on the Love of Our Country*.[7] He found his text in Psalm 72: "Pray for the peace of Jerusalem. They shall prosper that love thee." Christian love of country was a noble passion, not false pride or chauvinism; it taught universal benevolence and friendliness to the · "general rights of man." Though self-interest had a proper

[6] C. Kegan Paul, *William Godwin, His Friends and Contemporaries* (2 vols., Boston, 1876), I, 61. Godwin gives the date as November 5.

[7] In its printed form, *A Discourse on the Love of our Country, delivered on November 4, 1789, at the meeting-house in the Old Jewry, to the Society for commemorating the Revolution in Great Britain. With an appendix, containing the Report of the Committee of the Society; an Account of the population of France; and the Declaration of Rights by the National Assembly of France* (London, 1789).

place in any moral system, men were also "citizens of the world." Christianity, morality, and reason combined to make love of country a principle of action that brought us to love our neighbors almost as ourselves.

The country in which prevailed truth, virtue, and liberty, Price continued, deserved the love of its citizens. Therefore, give the people "just ideas of civil government, and let them know that it is an expedient for gaining protection against injury and defending their rights, and it will be impossible for them to submit to governments which, like most of those now in the world, are usurpations on the rights of men, and little better than contrivances for enabling the few to oppress the many." Moreover, "Set religion before them as a rational service, consisting not in any rights and ceremonies, but in worshipping God with a pure heart and practising righteousness from the fear of his displeasure and the apprehension of a future righteous judgement, and that gloomy and cruel superstition will be abolished which has hitherto gone under the name of religion, and to the support of which civil government has been perverted." Some teachers, such as Milton, Locke, and Montesquieu, did these things, and from their writings stemmed "those revolutions in which every friend of man is now exulting."

These sentiments introduced Price's specific recommendations. First, he demanded religious reforms. The continuance of the "application of civil power to the support of particular modes of faith . . . obstructs human improvement, and perpetuates error." In addition to disestablishment of the Anglican Church, he wanted the removal of all religious and political disabilities upon non-Anglicans. If this frightened Anglicans, Price's political program profoundly disturbed all who believed in the perfection of the unreformed constitution. Liberty, he said, had most often been lost because of the apathy of the people.[8] Only vigilance held kings in check; royal re-

8 This sentiment resembled the expression of Demosthenes in his *Second Philippic* —"there is one common safeguard in the nature of prudent men, which is a good security for all, especially for democracies against despots.

bellions against the rights of subjects worked more mischief than popular uprisings against rulers. Remember, "Civil governors are properly the servants of the public; and a King is no more than the first servant of the public, created by it, maintained by it, and responsible to it." If Price should address the king of England, he could say nothing more fitting than "I honour you not only as my King, but as almost the only lawful king in the world, because the only one who owes his crown to the choice of his people." The consciousness of their sovereign authority, however, never excused lawlessness and disrespect of people for their legally constituted rulers. On the other hand, rulers who forgot that their power was a trust were enemies of the country. People who loved their country were obligated to defend it from all enemies, foreign or domestic.

A man who loved his country ought to pray for it; therefore, said Price, this assemblage should thank God for the Revolution of 1688. "By a bloodless victory, the fetters which despotism had long been preparing for us were broken; the rights of the people were asserted, a tyrant expelled, and a Sovereign of our own choice appointed in his room." Protestant Dissenters had a special reason for rejoicing, because the revolution asserted for them, and for everyone: "First: The right to liberty of conscience in religious matter. Secondly: The right to resist power when abused. And, Thirdly: The right to chuse our own governors; to cashier them for misconduct; and to frame a government for ourselves."

Here Price connected 1689 and 1789. Dissenters must strive to enlarge mere toleration into real religious freedom. The Revolution Society ought to work to strengthen the foundation of civil liberty. Though reform in England might be delayed "till the acquisition of a pure and equal representation by other countries (while we are mocked with the shadow) kindles our shame," yet the moment was at hand to

---

What do I mean? Mistrust. Keep this, hold to this; preserve this only, and you can never be injured."

resume the work interrupted by the defeat of Pitt's bill in 1785.

Price concluded his sermon by linking the French Revolution with the cause of further reform in England. This relationship at first stimulated reform activity, and then gave to the English government, as the French Revolution moved into its radical stages, excuses for suppressing brutally and thoroughly the reform movement for almost the duration of the Napoleonic Wars. Price's peroration was the high point of his sermon. He caught fire describing the visions he saw.

> I have lived to see the rights of men better understood than ever; and nations panting for liberty, which seemed to have lost the idea of it.—I have lived to see Thirty millions of people, indignant and resolute, spurning at slavery, and demanding liberty with an irresistible voice; their king led in triumph, and an arbitrary monarch surrendering himself to his subjects. . . . I see the ardor for liberty catch and spreading. . . . Behold, the light you have struck out, after setting America free, reflected to France, and there kindled into a blaze that lays despotism in ashes, and warms and illuminates Europe!

And last, a note of warning, "Restore to mankind their rights; and consent to the correction of abuses, before they and you are destroyed together."

The sermon was an oratorical triumph. In stirring language Price communicated to his audience not only his thoughts, but his feelings as well. Then, after resting at home for several hours, Price went to the London Tavern where the society was holding its dinner under the chairmanship of Earl Stanhope. The society, still enthusiastic, sent a congratulatory address to the French National Assembly, through the good offices of the Duke de la Rochefoucauld. Who more than Dr. Price was fitted to move the address? His language and sentiments were those of his sermon.

> The Society for commemorating the Revolution in GREAT BRITAIN, disdaining national partialities, and rejoicing

in every triumph of liberty and justice over arbitrary power, offer to the National Assembly of FRANCE their congratulations on the Revolution in that country, and on the prospect it gives to the first two kingdoms in the world of a common participation in the blessings of civil and religious liberty.

They cannot help adding their ardent wishes of a happy settlement of so important a Revolution, and at the same time expressing the particular satisfaction with which they reflect on the tendency of the glorious example given in FRANCE to encourage other nations to assert the inalienable rights of mankind, and thereby to introduce a general reformation in the governments of EUROPE, and to make the world free and happy.

Price was exhausted when, after one of the busiest and most exciting days of his life, he returned home that night. If he slept at all, he must have dropped off to sleep thinking of the dawning of the era of the brotherhood of man.

The *Discourse* was published immediately. Two editions appeared before the end of 1789, four more in 1790, and the pamphlet was reprinted in Boston, Dublin, and in Paris in translation. To the original sermon was added an appendix stating three propositions which were "the fundamental principles of the Society." These were: "That all civil and political authority is derived from the people. That the abuse of power justifies resistance. That the rights of private judgement, liberty of conscience, trial by jury, the freedom of the press, and the freedom of election ought ever to be held sacred and inviolable." The appendix also recommended the establishment of societies in other English cities to maintain a correspondence with one another as part of their joint endeavors to promote these three principles. In 1790, published separately from the *Discourse,* appeared two editions of *Additions to Dr. Price's Discourse . . . containing communications from France, occasioned by the Congratulatory Address of the Revolution Society to the National Assembly of France; with the answers to them.*

The pamphlet had a varied reception. Characteristic of the hostile attitude was the review in the *Gentleman's Magazine* for December, 1789. Price was a unique person, the writer admitted, "a man of talents to take any side,—a man of disappointed vanity to desert any." As for the *Discourse*, "It is the dotage of Dr. P."—the sentiment "puerile," the style "vapid," and the doctrine that of an "Incendiary in civil, schismatic in religious, rights!" The reformers, of course, praised Price's ideas, which were also theirs. Various constitutional societies, among them those of Cambridge, Norwich, and Manchester, framed public expressions of their regard for Price. The Constitutional Society of London on December 16 at a dinner attended by him accepted a toast to "Dr. Price, the Friend of the Universe." This title or its variation, the "Friend of Mankind," was a usual appellation for Price by this time, and it has been used ever since. In July, 1937, a bronze plaque was unveiled in the public library of Bridgend. The inscription calls Price "Philosopher . Preacher . Actuary . Cfaill Dynolryw" (Friend of Humanity).[9]

In France, Price was hailed by the Revolutionaries as a hero. "His name was a passport to the best society of revolutionary Paris, and to be known as his friend was to be sure of a welcome in circles where in 1790 and 1791 the chiefs of the movement were to be met."[10] Numerous French societies acclaimed him. The Friends of the Constitution of Montpellier wrote to the Revolutionary Society "Nos coeurs ont tressaillés aux idées consolantes de Price et de Sheridan."[11] A society at Vire wrote, "dans toute les parties de la France, les noms de Milord Stanhope, du Docteur Price, de R. Sheridan et de tous les membres de la Société de Londres ont été répétés avec attendrissement."[12] Communications came to Price from other French organizations at Aix, Alais, Amiens, Arras,

[9] The ceremony was described in the Cardiff *Western Mail*, July 22, 1937, and Dr. Roland Thomas unveiled the plaque. Miss H. J. Williams, librarian of the Bridgend County Library, supplied the photograph of the plaque and a copy of the newspaper article.

[10] Clayden, *Early Life of Samuel Rogers*, 119-20.

[11] Lincoln, *English Dissent*, 58.   [12] *Ibid.*, 58. n. 4.

Auxerre, Bordeaux, Brest, Calais, Chalon-sur-Mer, Cherbourg, Cresy, Dijon, Grenoble, and so on through the alphabet. Many Frenchmen visited London during the first two years of the revolution, and Price, always seeking news about French affairs, learned much from those who sought his acquaintance. On May 27, 1790, the American minister to France, Gouverneur Morris, dined at Shelburne's London house, where among the guests were several liberal Frenchmen and "Doctor Price . . . who is one of the Liberty-mad People."[13]

By this time the *Discourse* was circulating in the United States. John Adams, to whom Price sent a copy, wrote a letter of thanks, and honest as always, he would not give it unqualified praise.[14] He admired Price's general sentiments, but he doubted the ability of the French to understand and to practice the true principles of civil liberty. "I have learned by awful experience to rejoice with trembling." Adams disliked the actions of the National Assembly regarding the church in France, and he expressed skepticism about the stability of a republic composed of thirty million atheists. The French talked too much about "equality of persons and property." With great prescience, and this disturbed Price a little, Adams feared that Europe might be in for a century of warfare "for want of a little attention to the true elements of the science of government." In a letter to Thomas Brand-Hollis, Adams voiced the same doubts.[15] "I am delighted with Dr. Price's sermon on patriotism; but there is a sentiment or two which I should explain a little." Like Burke, he feared the tyranny of a multitude as much as the tyranny of a despot or of oligarchs. Benjamin Rush had no qualifications to make. He thought the *Discourse* was "pregnant with noble sentiments."[16]

Horace Walpole, who of course detested Price and his philosophy, was not perturbed by the possibilities that incendiaries might start trouble in England. Snob that he was,

[13] Beatrix Cary Davenport (ed.), *A Diary of the French Revolution* (2 vols., Boston, 1932), I, 528.
[14] Adams (ed.), *Works of John Adams*, IX, 563-65, letter of April 19, 1790.
[15] *Ibid.*, 570.   [16] M.H.S P. (1903), 374.

PLAQUE ON THE BRIDGEND PUBLIC LIBRARY

he betrayed a remarkable confidence in the good sense of the common people that more properly should have been the foundation of a strong democratic belief. Writing on July 23, 1790, to Mary Berry, he described a recent journey through the English countryside. The houses and farms were so neat and orderly "that every five miles were an answer to Dr. Price and Lord Stanhope."[17]

While Price was being enthusiastically toasted and frequently, though not yet heavily or bitterly, castigated, a terrible storm was brewing. England's mightiest penman was preparing a verbal damnation of Price, of the reformers of England, and of the revolution in France. A month before Price preached his sermon, Burke expressed doubts about the wisdom of the proceedings in the National Assembly to M. de Menonville, a member of that body.[18] He wrote, "I see some people here are willing that we should become their [Voltaire's and Rousseau's] scholars too, and reform our State on the French model. They have begun; and it is high time for those who wish to preserve *morem majorum* to look about them." The *Discourse* confirmed Burke's apprehensions. He began seriously the labor of counteracting such political doctrines.

During the first winter of the revolution Burke worked hard on his book, revising and polishing without diluting the emotionalism that pervaded his original, feverish draft. On February 20, 1790, he wrote to Philip Francis concerning some proof sheets which Francis had read and criticized.[19] Agreeing with him about the "vileness" of a controversy with the reformers in England and the National Assembly in France, Burke insisted that the worthiness of the cause justified exposing himself to abuse.

> But I intend no controversy with Dr. Price, or Shelburne, or any other of their set. I mean to set in full view the

[17] Lewis (ed.), *Correspondence of Horace Walpole*, XI, 98.

[18] James Prior, *Memoir of the Life and Character of the Right Hon. Edmund Burke* (3d ed., London, 1839), 327.

[19] Earl Fitzwilliam and Richard Bourke (eds.), *Correspondence of the Right Honourable Edmund Burke* (4 vols., London, 1844), IV, 134-41.

danger from their wicked principles and their black hearts.
I intend to state the true principles of our constitution
in church and state, upon grounds opposite to theirs. . . .
I mean to do my best to expose them to the hatred, ridi-
cule and contempt of the whole world; as I always shall
expose such calumniators, hypocrites, sowers of sedition,
and approvers of murder and all its triumphs. When I
have done that, they may have the field to themselves; and
I care very little how they triumph over me, since I hope
they will not be able to draw me at their heels, and carry
my head in triumph on their poles.

It is difficult to understand how Burke thought he could avoid
controversy with those he attacked.

In fact, a controversy, of which Price was a central figure,
had already begun between the advocates and the opponents
of reform in England. This earlier criticism of Price had a
certain tolerant impatience that disappeared after the publication of Burke's *Reflections on the Revolution in France.*
Bitterness, exacerbated by the fears Burke's book inspired,
became henceforth a dominant passion of those who rushed to
support the established order in England. Panicky opprobrium
took the place of reasoned argument. English opinion became
sharply divided after Burke's *Reflections* crystallized the
thoughts of many persons who hitherto had not made up
their minds about the revolution in France and reform in
England, or only mildly disapproved. Most of the people
of the middle ground decided in favor of the conservative
doctrines pronounced by Burke, for Englishmen were no longer
in doubt that between events in France and ideas in England
was a direct and intimate connection.

In the meantime, Price and the reformers continued optimistically on their way. On July 14, 1790, fell the first anniver-
sary of the taking of the Bastille, and a group, some of them
members of the Revolution Society, met at the Crown and
Anchor Tavern to celebrate the memory of that glorious event.
Price attended, made an ardent speech, and proposed a noble
toast. The toast, in fact, was the climax of his address. Since
1688, he said, England fought five wars that loaded the

nation with a crushing burden of debt. Another war would bring still greater miseries. But wars were no longer necessary. There was a disposition in France toward peace and an alliance with England. This sentiment was the first fruit of the revolution, which promised "a new and better order in human affairs." The English example stimulated the French to seek freedom; now they had attained it and their achievement encouraged the people of England to enlarge their liberties. The most intriguing possibility of this new era was an alliance between the two countries. Such an alliance would have a magnetic power that would draw into it Holland, the other countries of Europe, and even the United States, so that "when alarms of war come, they will be able to say to contending nations, *Peace*, and there will be *peace*." To this end Price proposed as a toast, "An alliance between France and Great Britain, for perpetuating peace, and making the world happy."[20] ·

Price described this meeting as a "very animating" one.[21] In his message to the Duke de la Rochefoucauld, he enclosed for the president of the district of Quimper in Bretagne an answer to a pleasing letter from the society of that district. Price also asked the Duke to send to a literary society at L'Orient an answer to a letter he had received from it.

Price's last public appearance at a reform gathering was his attendance at the meeting of the Revolution Society on November 4, 1790. He presided in the absence of Earl Stanhope, and he proposed an ambitious toast: "The Parliament of Britain—May it become a National Assembly."[22] Opponents of reform would have thought the toast ominous except that the meeting was smaller and less enthusiastic than the one of the preceding year. The St. James *Chronicle* gloated.[23] If next year's secession was as large as this year's, the society could meet in a smaller room. But Price's enthusiasm had not waned.

20 Rutt, *Priestley*, II, 79-80 n.
21 M.H.S.P. (1903), 376. This source does not give the date of the letter nor the name of the person to whom it was directed, but Rutt, *Priestley*, II, 87-88 n., identifies the recipient as the Duke de la Rochefoucauld.
22 Thomas, *Price*, 135.
23 Quoted in Lewis (ed.), *Correspondence of Horace Walpole*, XI, 135, n. 38.

Despite his infirmities, according to Horace Walpole, he climbed upon a table to give his toast.[24] This dinner of the Revolution Society took place just after the appearance of Burke's *Reflections*, of which the members took sarcastic notice by toasting its author. "If Mr. Burke be ever prosecuted for such a libel on the constitution, may his impeachment last as long as that of Mr. Hastings."[25]

The tremendous reception given the *Reflections* was due in part to the eagerness with which people had awaited its publication. The London *Chronicle* for November 2, 1790, could not remember when a forthcoming book had aroused such curiosity as Burke's. By the end of November, twelve thousand copies were sold. Defenders of the old order boasted a champion who showed the reformers and the friends of the French Revolution in their true colors. Horace Walpole gleefully noted that "Dr. Price, who had whetted his ancient talons last year to no purpose, has had them all drawn by Burke, and the Revolution Club is as much exploded as the Cock Lane Ghost."[26] Catherine Macaulay Graham, a friend of Price and in Walpole's words the leader of the "Amazonian allies" of the reformers, took a surprisingly objective view of the effect of Burke's *Reflections*. She said the book clarified the issues of the controversy, and henceforth there would be two sides and no middle party. One group looked upon the revolution with "exultation and rapture," the other with "indignation and scorn."[27] No quarter was allowed in the struggle that ensued.

A pamphlet war, the literary expression of the movement for political reform, broke out after the publication of the *Reflections*. Price's *Discourse* stated the reformers' side of the argument. Burke's *Reflections*, prompted in part by the

[24] *Ibid.*, 135.

[25] London *Chronicle*, November 6, 1790. The trial of Hastings, led by Burke, was already two and a half years old, and it was not to be concluded until April, 1795.

[26] Lewis (ed.), *Correspondence of Horace Walpole*, XI, 146, letter to Mary Berry, November 18, 1790.

[27] London *Chronicle*, December 4, 1790.

words of Price, expressed eloquently the ideas, the prejudices, and the fears of those who opposed constitutional change. Others jumped into the dispute, and after the death of Price, Tom Paine, because of his authorship of the *Rights of Man* and the antimonarchial views given therein, became to the conservatives the living symbol of the horrors of extreme democracy. On October 4, 1792, the *Morning Chronicle* reported that never before had such a flood of pamphlets swept over England.

Though Burke worried about the revolution and its possible consequences before Price delivered his *Discourse,* he was not positively alarmed until Price spoke. He confessed to a feeling of "uneasiness" because Price's sermon was intended to connect "the affairs of France with those of England, by drawing us into an imitation of the conduct of the National Assembly."[28] Likewise, Burke had previously paid little attention to the Revolution Society until deceitfully holding itself up in a kind of "public capacity" as an organ for expressing to the French the sentiments of the English people, it became really dangerous. The thoughts contained in the society's "Address" originated "in the principles of the sermon" preached by Price, a sermon in which some "good moral and religious sentiments" were "mixed up with a sort of porridge of various political opinions and reflections." The important thing was that "the Revolution in France is the grand ingredient in the caldron." The "Address" was moved by the person who preached the *Discourse,* and it was passed by men "who came reeking from the effects of the sermon."

But it was less Price than what he symbolized that disturbed Burke. "I looked on that sermon as the public declaration of a man much connected with literary caballers and intriguing philosophers, with political theologians and theological politicians both at home and abroad. I know they set him up as a sort of oracle; because, with the best intentions in the world, he naturally *philippizes,* and chants his prophetic song in exact unison with their designs."[29] The sermon contained ideas that

[28] "Reflections," *Works,* III, 242.   [29] *Ibid.,* 245.

undermined the foundations of the English constitution and placed the throne in a "dangerous, illegal, and unconstitutional position."

Burke examined carefully the Revolution of 1688 because Price made it his point of departure for demanding further reforms. Price thought it the initial step in the liberalization of political life in England, where Burke, like the conservative Whigs, looked upon it with an air of finality. He tried to demonstrate that Price read into the Revolutionary Settlement meanings which were not present in the minds of the men who made that revolution. Perhaps he was right in the narrow sense, but Price's views were the ones destined to be carried along in the stream of English history.

Price had asserted that the king of England "owes his crown to the choice of his people," as Burke put it. The Revolution Settlement, said Burke, only confirmed the hereditary criterion. Obviously Price and Burke were not standing on common ground. Price never claimed anything so absurd as Burke suggested when he said the king "holds his crown in contempt of the choice of the Revolution Society, who have not a single vote for the king amongst them." Price meant nothing more than that the king ruled by the tacit consent of the people. Burke admitted the deviation from the direct line of hereditary succession in 1688, but excused it on the grounds of extreme necessity. He was unfair in accusing Price of asserting that at any time and for any reason the people could assert their sovereignty, cashier their governors, and choose new ones. Price meant simply that in the final analysis the power to do these things resided in the nation. Actually, in admitting that such an action as that of 1688 was justifiable by extreme necessity, Burke was agreeing with Price. The controversy between them really boiled down to a matter of degree, of the respective interpretations to be placed upon the word necessary.

Price blundered in using the word misconduct when he spoke of cashiering rulers. The word was not clear in its limitations. Burke properly denied that dethronement for

Caricature by J. Gillray

SMELLING OUT A RAT OR THE ATHEISTICAL-REVOLUTIONIST DIS-
TURBED IN HIS MIDNIGHT "CALCULATIONS" VIDE—A TROUBLED
CONSCIENCE

mere indiscretion was acceptable, but again he was deliberately and obstinately refusing to understand Price's meaning. His own definition of the reason for the Revolution of 1688 would be quite acceptable to Price—"a grave and overruling necessity obliged them [the opponents of James II] to take the step they took, and took with infinite reluctance."

As to the right "to frame a government for ourselves," Burke's case was built upon his philosophy of conservatism, that in turn grew out of a strong sense of historical continuity. A government could not spring out of the Jovian brows of any group of men, even one so capable as the National Assembly. It evolved through centuries of experience and was shaped by circumstances and the wisdom of generations of men. Occasional modifications which conformed to existing principles were beneficial, but violent departures from the past were dangerous. The larger part of the *Reflections* amplified this conservatism as it related to the reform movement in England, to the French Revolution, and to human affairs in any period of history. This is why the *Reflections* has remained an important and relevant book.

But in its immediate context, the *Reflections* distorted Price's ideas. Price did not want to destroy the British constitutional system or to build a fundamentally different one upon new foundations. The reforms he wanted were implicit in the Revolution of 1688. They derived from the principle of the sovereignty of the people, upon which that revolution was based. Price desired a wider suffrage and more equitable distribution of representation in Parliament, while leaving unchanged the formal structure of king, Lords, and Commons. He abhorred violent revolutions; nor did he think, because of what had been achieved by the Revolution of 1688, that forceful measures were necessary.

Yet there had been two revolutions within living memory, and Price's philosophy underlay them. In upholding the sovereignty of the people, Price made of the right of revolution a positive right. Though he denied that revolution was a matter of rights, Burke recognized that revolutions occurred.

A revolution should always be "a question (like all other questions of state) of dispositions, and of means, and of possible consequences." That, in fact, was Burke's real quarrel with the revolutionaries. He believed they were too ready to assert the violation of rights, and too little cognizant of consequences. Revolutionaries like Price were too quick to go from obedience to resistance. The line between is "faint, obscure, and not easily definable. It is not a single act or a single event which determines it. Governments must be abused and deranged indeed, before it can be thought of; and the prospect of the future must be as bad as the experience of the past. . . . with or without right, a revolution will be the very last resource of the thinking and the good." With this admission, Burke conceded that revolutions were, under certain circumstances, justifiable. Price would agree. He might have been just a little readier to step across the line dividing obedience from resistance, but the act would bear just as heavy a responsibility for him as for Burke. Price would have agreed with his opponent that resistance was justified only by "a necessity that is not chosen, but chooses, a necessity paramount to deliberation, that admits no discussion and demands no evidence."

Having dealt with the English Revolution, Burke then considered the one in France, keeping always in mind the English situation and the possible reaction upon it of events in France. He saw more profoundly into the meaning of the French Revolution than did any of his contemporaries, including Goethe, whose much quoted statement concerning the battle of Valmy rings empty. Burke considered the revolution to be a movement of ideas. Out of it was being generated a new spirit which, impossible to confine within political boundaries or geographical frontiers, might work a fundamental change in European society. The French Revolution, to Burke, was of the same character as the Protestant Reformation. In the end, his opposition became a holy crusade against Jacobinism, atheism, and regicide which would, if not checked, overturn the ancient order of society that he loved.

So Price, this mild man, was dangerous. His philosophy was incendiary; he symbolized and spoke for a group of men in England who, sympathetic to the French Revolution, would let loose the tides of organic change.

CHAPTER XIV

THE LAST YEAR

FROM the publication of Burke's *Reflections* until his own death six months later, Price remained a silent spectator of events in France and England. He did not reply to Burke, but his friends and allies directed some forty pamphlets against the *Reflections*. Some defended Price directly, while all advocated political reforms.[1] Among the champions of Price were his old friends, Capel Lofft and Christopher Wyvill, colleagues in the reform movement of the preceding decade. Wyvill entitled one of his pamphlets *A Defense of Dr. Price, and the Reformers of England*.[2] Joseph Priestley, as one might expect, rushed into the controversy fresh from a reading of the *Reflections*. Price read Priestley's reply in manuscript, and it was published at Birmingham in 1791 under the title *Letters to the Right Honourable Edmund Burke, occasioned by his Reflections on the Revolution in France*.

After Tom Paine brought out his *Rights of Man*, conservative attacks centered on him. The opponents of reform, however, did not forget Price. Though Paine's republicanism was much more radical than most reform ideas, conservatives made no distinctions among reformers, branding all of them indiscriminately as incendiaries. Long after Price was dead, scurrilous attacks were made against him. The *Anti-Jacobin*,

[1] Carl B. Cone, "Pamphlet Replies to Burke's *Reflections*," *Southwestern Social Science Quarterly*, XXVI (1945-1946), 22-34, and "English Reform Ideas during the French Revolution," *ibid.*, XXVII (1946-1947), 368-84.
[2] (York, 1792).

a periodical that did not appear until 1797, castigated Price as severely as if he were still alive. Much bitter doggerel verse appeared. Some samples illustrate the spirit in which it was written.

> Let our vot'ries then follow the glorious advice,
> In the Gunpowder Legacy left us by Price,
> Inflammable matter to place grain by grain
> And blow up the State with the torch of Tom Paine![3]

John Wolcot, who wrote under the name of Peter Pindar, defamed everybody. In "The Louisiad" he described Madame Discord and her Cell. Speaking of the pictures in her dwelling,

> There, in respect to Kings not over-nice,
> That Revolution-sinner Doctor Price:
> Whose Labours, in a most uncourtly style,
> Win not, like *gentle* Burke's, the Royal smile.[4]

Wolcot's poem called "The Rights of Kings, or Loyal Odes to Disloyal Academicians" was motivated by the refusal of the Royal Society to accede to the king's desires in a certain election.

> Stanhope, perchance, will clasp you in his arms;
> And Price's Ghost, with eloquence charms,
> Will, from his tomb, up-springing, sound applause.[5]

Later in the same poem, speaking of the disgraces heaped upon the French king,

> Lo, you took advice,
> I'm sure, from that Arch-devil, Doctor Price,
> And Stanhope, who so praise the French and clap,
> For catching Kings, like Polecats, in a trap.[6]

Two months after Price's death, Horace Walpole sent to Mary Berry the kind of nasty letter he wrote so well. He spoke

---

[3] Quoted in Lincoln, *English Dissent*, 30, n. 2.
[4] *The Works of Peter Pindar* (5 vols., London, 1812), I, 253.
[5] *Ibid.*, II, 392.   [6] *Ibid.*, 407-409.

of the brutalities inflicted upon the French royal family after the flight to Varennes, brutalities "which nobody but the French and Dr. Price could be so shameless as to enjoy."[7]

This kind of abuse was also directed at Price while he was still living, but it never bothered him. During his last winter Price devoted himself complacently to his personal affairs. He learned sadly how John Howard, "my intimate friend from early life," had died of disease at Cherson, Russia, on January 20, 1790. Before his death, Howard ordered his servant to send back his notes for Price and Aikin to prepare for publication. Price was too ill to assist. Aikin did the work, publishing the notes as an appendix to the *Lazarettos*.

About the same time, Price heard of Franklin's death. Benjamin Rush, who for some years had been Price's most faithful American correspondent, described the last weeks of Franklin's life, his death, and his funeral. On June 19, 1790, Price replied.[8] He "had just finished reading an account of his [Franklin's] life which he had sent to be perused by me and my friend R. B. Vaughan. . . . I have been long happy in his friendship, and I have always thought myself honoured by it. The account which he has left of his life will shew, in a striking example, how a man by talents, industry, and integrity, may rise from obscurity, to the first eminence, and consequence in the world."

The deaths of these old friends re-emphasized the infirmities which Price had forgotten in the excitement of the early revolution. He spent two months sea-bathing at Bridgend, not returning to London until October, 1790. He had extended his vacation "in hopes of obtaining a recruit of health and spirits." He gave a little thought to writing his memoirs, for he was reading in manuscript those of Priestley, who encouraged him to undertake the task. Price never got beyond a brief sketch of his later years. He worked on a fifth edition of his *Reversionary Payments*, but had to leave it for William

---

[7] Lewis (ed.), *Correspondence of Horace Walpole*, XI, 299, letter of June 29, 1791.

[8] Rush Manuscripts.

Morgan to finish. He also continued to correspond with old friends, most frequently with Priestley. Despite physical weakness and pains in his right leg, he preached every Sunday at the Gravel-Pit Meeting House. Constantly he watched the progress of the French Revolution and the reform movement.

Early in February, 1791, standing bareheaded in bad weather, he caught cold while officiating at a funeral in Bunhill-Fields. He recovered slightly, resumed his preaching, attended another funeral, and the cold returned. Yet on Sunday, February 20, he insisted on preaching. This was his last sermon. By Wednesday he had a high fever. Medical attention gave him a little relief, and he was able to go out once in a carriage.

Price's friends showed great anxiety; "his door was surrounded with anxious enquiries after his health." Priestley's letters to Lindsey chronicled Price's illness. On March 7, Priestley had just heard of the consequences of the neglected cold; two days later he learned there were hopes for Price; on March 11 he rejoiced that Price seemed to be out of immediate danger; on March 25 there was a chance for recovery, though there would be danger for a while.[9] The London *Chronicle* for March 26-29 reported that "Dr. Price lies dangerously ill at his house in Hackney. His complaint is a strangury."[10] By April there was less possibility of recovery, and Priestley, who always received his information a little late, worried. He wrote that Price had always been concerned about getting the stone after his good friend James Burgh had suffered so much from it.[11]

Horace Walpole, having learned of the serious illness of Mirabeau, who died on April 2, wrote to Mary Berry two days later, "Dr. Price is dying also—fortunate omens for those who hope to die in their beds too."[12]

[9] Rutt, *Priestly*, II, 102, 104, 105, 107.
[10] Quoted in Lewis (ed.), *Correspondence of Horace Walpole*, XI, 239, n. 22.
[11] Rutt, *Priestley*, II, 109.
[12] Lewis (ed.), *Correspondence of Horace Walpole*, XI, 239.

Price lingered for two more weeks, maintaining his equanimity to the end. On April 18 he became much weaker. Shortly after midnight he died, "praising God for his goodness."[13]

Price's death brought "that unaffected sorrow which evidently proves the loss of a truly worthy man."[14] His friends insisted upon a public funeral, though they knew that was contrary to the directions Price had left. The Revolution and Constitutional societies came in a body; most of Price's dissenting friends were there, and so were the Duke of Portland and Earl Stanhope. Six dissenting clergymen, among them Priestley, bore the casket to the grave in which lay Mrs. Price and Uncle Samuel. Kippis preached at the cemetery, and on May 1 Priestley delivered the funeral oration at the Gravel-Pit Meeting House.

Their eulogies, like those that came from various societies in France, seem extravagant, but they were not unmerited despite the verdict of history. For, unless he has the rare qualities of a Franklin, and some good fortune, a person such as Price is hardly likely to catch public fancy and win a hero's laurels in a revolutionary age.

[13] M.H.S.P. (1910), 634, letter of Thomas Brand-Hollis to Joseph Willard. November 4, 1791.
[14] *Gentleman's Magazine*, LXI (1791), part 1, pp. 389-90.

BIBLIOGRAPHICAL NOTE

The materials, both primary and secondary, used in writing this book are indicated in the footnotes, but an explanatory note concerning the most important ones may be in order. The works of Price, which are analyzed in the appropriate places in the text, are basic.

The largest collection of Price's correspondence is contained in the *Proceedings of the Massachusetts Historical Society*, Second Series, XVII (1903), 262-378. In this collection are letters from and to Price during the years 1767-1790.

The Chatham Papers, G. D. 8/169 and G. D. 8/275, in the Public Record Office, London, contain letters and papers of Price relating to the national debt and the Sinking Fund, for the years 1782-1786.

In the Rush Manuscripts in the custody of the Library Company of Philadelphia, Broad and Christian Streets, Philadelphia, are seven letters from Price to Benjamin Rush, during the years 1783-1790. These letters concern mainly American affairs, and are valuable for suggestions of Price's American connections and his interest in the political problems of the United States.

The Shelburne Papers in the William L. Clements Library, Ann Arbor, Michigan, contain less Price material than one might expect, considering the length and the intimacy of the association between Price and Shelburne. The most valuable volume in the collection is 117, entitled "Revenue Notes & Calculations by Dr. Price." In this volume are a score of financial papers written by Price over the years 1761-1789, dealing with a variety of matters ranging from the window tax and duties on herring to the national debt and the Sinking Fund. Apart from this volume, the Shelburne Papers have little significant material for the purpose of this book. Yet, because of the nature of the relationship between Price and Shelburne, one would not dare write a biography of Price without consulting them. This collection is the same one often referred to in English bibliographies as the "Lansdowne" collection, after the later title of the Earl of Shelburne.

Among miscellaneous manuscripts, of no great value, there is one letter by Price in the Benjamin Vaughan Papers, Vol. 5, Clements Library; one letter from Franklin to Price in the Miscellaneous

Collection, Clements Library; one letter from Price to an unidenti-
fied person, in the R. B. Adam Collection, formerly in the Rush
Rhees Library, University of Rochester; four letters by Price in the
British Museum, Additional Manuscripts—28,541 F. 40; 30,872 F.
266; 34,417 F. 12; and 34,420 F. 29—and one letter from Price to
Barlow in the Joel Barlow Papers, Box 2, Harvard Library.

The previous biographers of Price, William Morgan and Roland
Thomas, have used none of these materials except the letters
printed in the *Proceedings of the Massachusetts Historical Society*,
which Morgan used while they were still in the custody of Price's
heirs. He also reprinted some of Price's financial papers in his
editions of the *Observations on Reversionary Payments*.

The periodical literature concerning Price is not extensive nor
valuable, but he is mentioned occasionally in the contemporary
publications and in some of the subsequent periodicals. The
memoirs and letters of persons who lived in Price's time, and the
biographies and secondary literature treating the era of Price, have
references to him. He is not discussed at length in any of them,
but the notices occur in a variety of works, indicating the ubiquitous
nature of his activities and contacts. He is to be found in the
company of many great men of his time, or is an acquaintance of
so many others, that one quickly gets the impression that Price
was well known in his own lifetime. Price is most frequently noticed
during the periods of the American and French revolutions, when
his political activities earned him so much attention.

INDEX